Succeed
for Yourself

3RD EDITION

RICHARD DENNY

**KOGAN
PAGE**

London and Philadelphia

For Dorothy.
A very special person whom I am proud to call my wife.

Throughout the book 'he' and 'she' are used liberally. If there is a proponderance of the masculine pronoun it is because the inadequacies of the English language do not provide a single personal pronoun suitable to refer to both sexes.

Publisher's note
Every possible effort has been made to ensure that the information contained in this book is accurate at the time of going to press, and the publishers and authors cannot accept responsibility for any errors or omissions, however caused. No responsibility for loss or damage occasioned to any person acting, or refraining from action, as a result of the material in this publication can be accepted by the editor, the publisher or any of the authors.

First published in 1997
Second edition 2002
Third edition 2006
This edition 2010

Kogan Page Limited
120 Pentonville Road
London N1 9JN
United Kingdom
www.koganpage.com

Kogan Page US
525 South 4th Street, #241
Philadelphia PA 19147
USA

ISBN 978 0 7494 5644 3

British Library Cataloguing in Publication Data

A CIP record for this book is available from the British Library.

Library of Congress Cataloging-in-Publication Data

Denny, Richard.
   Succeed for yourself : unlock your potential for success and happiness / Richard Denny.
      p. cm.
   ISBN 978-0-7494-5644-3
   1.   Success. 2.   Self-actualization (Psychology) 3.   Success in business.   I. Title.
BF637.S8D374 2009
650.1—dc22
                                 2009022277

Typeset by Saxon Graphics Ltd, Derby
Printed and bound in India by Replika Press Pvt Ltd

Contents

About the Author

Richard Denny is one of the United Kingdom's leading authorities on winning business and selling. He has improved the skills of more than one million people worldwide with his teachings, books, certificated courses and sales diplomas.

Richard is chairman of the Richard Denny Group, which specializes in business training and executive recruitment. He is also non-executive chairman of three other companies.

Richard Denny is the most inspirational business speaker in the United Kingdom. He is probably unique in that his presentations not only motivate, inspire and educate; his audiences also take away highly practical ideas that achieve enhanced performance. He is so confident that he guarantees to get an outstanding result. If not, his fee is refundable. You can't expect better than that (and it has never happened to date).

He has sold and marketed in the Middle East, where his products included steel, cement, Yugoslavian lamb and electronic equipment. With all this vast experience he was continually being asked to speak to and advise others, and this led to the Richard Denny Group being formed.

Over the past 20 years Richard has become a legend on the international speaking circuit. He gave his 2000th presentation in 2008. The Richard Denny Group is recognized as being at the forefront of business training on selling, leadership and management, customer care and business growth.

Richard has authored and presented over 40 training videos/CDs and 50 audio programmes. He is the author and presenter of three audio albums. His six books – *Selling to Win, Succeed for Yourself, Motivate to Win, Communicate to Win, Winning New Business* and *Successful Selling Skills* – are international best-sellers, selling into 46 countries and translated into 26 languages. *Selling to Win* has become required reading for anybody who wishes to aspire to becoming a sales professional, and the book is probably the world's best-seller on this subject.

Richard is the creator and founder of the British Professional Sales Diploma and the British Leadership & Management Diploma. He is also chairman of a telecommunications company in the United Kingdom.

He is a broadcaster, writer, married to Dorothy with six sons, and is an enthusiastic player of numerous sports. His presentations are liberally illustrated with anecdotes, people stories and of course that delightful Denny humour. Richard has the uncanny ability to delight any audience, probably because he talks common sense and has the knack of being a brilliant communicator. Apart from his experience as a keynote speaker, he also acts as a conference chairman and facilitator.

The Richard Denny Group
1 Cotswold Link
Moreton-in-Marsh
Gloucestershire GL56 0JU
Tel: +44 (0)1608 812424
Fax: +44 (0)1608 651638
Email: success@denny.co.uk
Website: www.denny.co.uk

Preface

This book is written for anyone who wants to achieve success in their life – and that must be *you*.

Every idea and thought I share with you here is based on my own personal experience and I can assure you that the practical advice I offer does work.

You have my personal guarantee that the principles I describe have brought success and happiness to me and my family and countless other people I have been fortunate enough to meet.

Now I want *you* to achieve the same – act upon what you read here and you too can unlock your potential for achieving success and happiness.

Words of praise for Richard Denny from members of the public who have been helped by his message

"I have just read Richard Denny's book *Succeed for Yourself* and have only one word to say about it – BRILLIANT!"
Margaret Jones, Fife

"Thank you for *Succeed for Yourself*, which I found truly awe-inspiring."
Nicola Faulkner, Executive PA, Chelmsford

"Firstly – thank you for writing *Succeed for Yourself*. Secondly – thank you for the book's good sound advice. I have put several of the recommendations into practice and can honestly say – it works!"
Carolyn Simpson, Medical Secretary, London

"Having read *Succeed for Yourself* last night, I leapt out of bed this morning full of ideas and raring to go. Thank you, I can't wait to pass it on."
Jane Fogerty, Wiltshire

"This book has transformed my life. From a bitter divorce, the loss of my home and financial ruin, I followed the advice in *Succeed for Yourself* and am now remarried, with a big new house and a small mortgage and a very large salary. Your advice really does work."
Kevin Young, Leeds

Introduction

One of the hardest concepts to define is success: it means quite different things to different people. Whatever it might mean to you, this book shows you how to achieve your ultimate desire to become a success in your own terms.

Sadly, the vision of success has been adulterated by the media through their continual thirst for sensation and glamour. The majority of us have been conditioned to believe that success is totally related to money. To have millions of pounds and the trappings of so-called success, such as Rolls-Royces, jets and holiday islands in paradise, is a common perception of what success is all about.

Moreover, success is held to be limited to those who reach the pinnacle in their chosen sport, or individuals who gain power in politics, industry or commerce. Parents who raise their children in a secure and happy home, or the managers who develop their staff to greater achievement and reward, often appear to be ignored.

WHAT IS SUCCESS?

Success for one person might be just to get the next meal, success for another might be to gain employment in a secure job, for another freedom from worry. Success for the vast majority of us, though, is to achieve our goals, to live in a state of happiness and to have respect from those around us. So you must be the judge and jury of what success means to you.

Success for one can be totally different from success for another. This was so well illustrated to me personally by the following, albeit rather sad, example:

Nicholas Darvas, 60 years of age, had been a partner in a dancing pair who had been incredibly successful throughout the world. He had amassed a personal fortune in excess of £1 million. He then invested astutely on the American stock exchange and made a further million pounds. He then wrote a book, *How to Make a Million on the Stock Exchange*, and added a few more millions to his ever-increasing wealth.

When I met him, he was single, living between the Dorchester Hotel in London, the George V in Paris and the Waldorf Hotel in New York. Through a series of discussions we had together, I found him to be a very bitter, sad and tragically lonely man. I pointed out to him his enormous financial wealth and what in those days I called success. He pointed out to me that in comparison to Bill Gates, the Barclay brothers, the Sultan of Brunei and the Duke of Westminster, he was not a success. He was worth but a pittance compared to the billions of dollars that they were worth. This may appear to be a rather negative example, but I use it as it has been of tremendous help and guidance to me in understanding how different people perceive success.

HOW THIS BOOK CAN HELP YOU

This book progresses in a logical order, but is nevertheless designed so that you can dip into the text and pull out bits that appeal to you personally.

I make no apology for the fact that many of the ideas and concepts in this book are not new. They are the great principle of success. In my thirst for a greater understanding of human achievement, I have learnt much through reading and listening to others wiser and more successful than me. I have personally used the ideas and concepts from, and have been fortunate to teach, the *Succeed for Yourself* system, and share it with countless other people who have also achieved great wealth and success. The many stories and analogies throughout the book are used to drive home ideas, systems and messages that lead to success.

This book is for everyone: for those who want to be a millionaire or billionaire, to be a sporting champion, to have and hold power, to be a great parent, to be an admired and respected person and for those who want the ultimate human desire – to be happy.

As you progress through the book, I examine the incredible power of the mind and the importance of investing in ourselves. I look at managing time, personal planning, self-management and setting goals. I provide methods for assessing strengths and weaknesses, methods for building self-image, and confidence techniques for visualizing success.

Each chapter is clearly set out and contains 'pocket reminders' at the end to reinforce the techniques throughout the book. I have tried and tested these principles and I can emphatically state that they work – the rest is up to you.

What is absolutely certain is that success is available and it awaits you!

> Tell me the old, old story
> Tell me the story often
> As I often forget so soon
> 'Tis old yet ever new

1

The Route to Success

Success, wealth and happiness guaranteed – too good to be true? Yet we are all born with these high expectations. They are unquestioned and unchallenged in our very early childhood, and then over the years from that positive beginning we become conditioned to be negative and our expectations lower.

Those three powerful words success, wealth and happiness have been cynically and sceptically dismissed by many as unavailable, not achievable and out of reach for all but the favoured few.

So, let me now attempt to re-establish those early, unquestioned positive expectations and take you on a journey to even greater success, wealth and happiness. Yes, let me state again, it is guaranteed for those who are prepared to follow the right route on this journey. You only have one run at this journey and it is not a practice run, it is the real thing.

Have you ever bought a flat-pack item and then tried to construct that product without following the instructions? Well, I confess I have, and then got into an almighty pickle and convinced myself pieces were missing, it wasn't complete and wasn't going to work anyhow. I learnt quickly that by following the instructions exactly not only did I get a positive result, but it was fairly easy and so much quicker.

I make this analogy with great seriousness, and as you start this incredible journey, follow the plan; do not vary it or take a short cut.

When you buy the flat pack they usually tell you what tools you need – screwdriver, hammer, etc. So, if you could go out and buy success instead of a flat-pack, what is success for you? If you are not sure at this stage I will help you in Chapter 7.

Whatever you do, do not make excuses – you know the old expression 'a bad workman always blames his tools'? I have heard people say, 'I'm too old', others, 'I'm too young', 'I didn't go to the right school', 'I didn't go to university' or even 'I was born under the wrong birth sign'. These are just a few of the thousands of excuses that are used to justify non-achievement.

I promise you that this book will help you achieve the success that you desire, as long as you remember that being an unhappy success is meaningless.

If you want to use the principles to create financial security or make the proverbial 'million', follow the stages. The vast majority of the principles are not new, but I know that they work because they have worked for me and for many others.

Do not dismiss them, undervalue them or treat them with cynicism. We all live in a world steeped in massive negativity, which can be seen in news programmes, the media and, of course, in other individuals. We are conditioned to become more cynical and sceptical about the enormous opportunities and possibilities in this incredible world in which we live and work.

WHAT IS HAPPINESS?

So let us examine what causes people to be happy.

Fundamentally, happiness is achieved in three ways: first, by having something to look forward to; secondly, by sharing; and thirdly, by making somebody else happy.

Looking forward to something

First, have something to look forward to. Have you ever experienced buying a new car? It might be brand new or second-hand. Your car is due to arrive in three days' time and you are excited. Two days to go, excitement increases, the arrival is getting closer. The day before, and perhaps even the night before, the excitement has increased even further. You may have difficulty going to sleep.

The new car arrives. That first day, of course, pleasure, enjoyment and happiness – lots of playing with the gadgetry and equipment, and every care is taken to make sure the car does not get dirty. Each time you park and walk away, you look back to make sure it hasn't moved! Two weeks later, how do you feel about the car? Yes, your attitude has changed – the car is now just another car. Pleasure rarely comes from the owning or the having – it comes from looking forward to owning it. This applies to almost anything, from holidays to watching a television programme to meeting a loved one to getting promoted.

We continually see on our TV screens the horrors of human conflict and deprivation. But surely the worst sight of all is a human face without hope. For you, my readers, there is *no* excuse for *you* not to have hope.

Sharing

Now let's take the second base for happiness: sharing. Imagine going out for a wonderful meal in a restaurant, perhaps ordering as a starter, large succulent Mediterranean prawns. Your second course could be a Chateaubriand steak prepared exactly to your own liking with some freshly prepared vegetables and trimmings. Your third course might be a marvellously light gateau or chocolate pudding. The whole meal accompanied with a vintage burgundy. What a meal! However, sit and eat that meal on your own and it's not much fun; certainly it creates very little happiness, and somehow the food does not taste the same as it would if you were sharing that meal with another person on the other side of the table to chat to.

So, sharing really does provide happiness. Now, many of us are fortunate enough to share our lives with a partner, while others find at some stage in their lives that, maybe through separation or bereavement, they are once again on their own. Does this mean the future is one of unhappiness? No, of course not. Most people have wonderful friendships and a wonderful family with whom they can share some of their time, joys and happiness. Many people gain tremendous happiness through sharing their life with a pet. The pet becomes a purpose for living, a reason for getting out of bed, and, of course, a great source of company for people on their own.

May I remind you of a saying that will be repeated later in this book... A joy that is shared is a joy that is doubled, a worry that is shared is a worry that is halved.

Making someone else happy

Third is making someone else happy. It is almost impossible not to be happy when you are making someone else happy. It is impossible not to be successful while helping to make someone else successful, and many successful business-people have proved, intentionally or otherwise, that by helping other people to be more financially successful, they have in turn enhanced their own wealth.

As a child, you look forward to birthdays and Christmas, obviously because these are times for surprises and presents. As you become more mature, the excitement and pleasure really come from the giving of these surprises and presents. Walk down a street sometime and smile – it is funny how people smile back. Notice how that makes you feel. As a parent, or as a manager, it is wonderful to be able to give somebody else some good news – you can get so much pleasure out of that simple exercise.

DON'T DISMISS THESE IDEAS

Cynics beware; dismiss these three principles at your peril. Your first reaction may be to question these ideas, but realize that a full understanding of happiness is one of the major areas upon which you should concentrate. What is sad is that this is not taught in our schools and universities, and even more concerning is that parents, in so many cases, have not passed this knowledge on to their offspring. It must therefore come as no surprise that so many seeking success are heading in completely the wrong direction.

Looking in the right direction

In 1994, the UK government launched for the first time a National Lottery. The build-up, advertising and promotion had unprecedented mass market appeal. On the first night that the lottery numbers were drawn, 25 million people watched the programme.

The programme placed a great deal of emphasis on the money that the eventual winner was going to receive. This hype turned into euphoria as the winning of millions of pounds was equated with success. The happiness that the winners would experience with those millions of pounds and what they could spend it on were stressed throughout, yet as the programme developed, I experienced ever greater sadness, not only for the winner, but also for the thousands upon thousands of more gullible people who would be influenced by this message.

The way to this vast fortune was not through work, endeavour, using one's brain, talent or skills, but through a lottery win – a chance – no different from a win on the horses, a Premium Bond, football pools, the dogs, blackjack, a fruit machine or any other chance win. It has been shown, time and time and time again, that the majority of those who win these huge sums of money do not achieve happiness. The first weeks, months and possibly year is a period of deciding what to spend and what to do next, and then the pressures take over. Families may be devastated by the begging and pleading of others, and the sharks appear with one new scheme after another to separate the money from the winner.

These people may also experience the loss of long-time friends for the simple reason that those friends now feel uncomfortable. They misguidedly believe that they have to compete. Their old friend may now have a new motor car, house, boat or whatever, but, deep inside, he or she is the same person. Family members may become jealous or competitive too.

I say all this with some heartfelt experience, not because I have won the lottery or had a major windfall, but in my very early thirties I made a great deal of money, through hard work and endeavour, and I experienced the trauma of some jealousies in my family. I also found that some of my longer-standing friends felt uncomfortable. I certainly did not allow myself to brag, but nevertheless, for most of us when we make money, and certainly at that age, we cannot help but buy the trappings – the luxury car and the lifestyle to go with it. It was a great learning experience.

Happiness as a result of your own efforts

When money is amassed through personal endeavour in whatever form, pleasure and happiness are achievable. In most cases when money is earnt through endeavour, it does not come in a single rush – the get-rich-quick scenario. The money comes gradually, which provides the individual with an opportunity to learn how to manage money. I do not oppose lotteries, but believe that people need a better under-standing of what such chance wins bring. For many people, the enormous benefit of a lottery, or that other great world-wide TV attraction *Who Wants to Be a Millionaire?*, is that it can provide hope, or an event to look forward to, and for that reason alone, many people who might otherwise be experiencing what could be described as a mundane exis-tence have a light at the end of the tunnel.

The power of hope

By contrast, for many years our television screens have been filled with horrific human conflict around the world. We have seen unimaginable pictures of human carnage and heinous crimes that defy belief. But may I suggest that the most desperate sight of all is not a starving body but a face without hope. We must always have hope; we cannot survive without it.

Let me give you an example of hope. My wife and I were shopping a while back when we overheard the following conversation (between a customer and a shop assistant):

'It's the lottery tonight, have you bought a ticket?', the shop assistant asked. 'Yes I have and I'm going to win', the customer replied, with a face that was now lit with excitement. 'If we win, we will completely decorate our lounge and get rid of all our dreadful carpet.' The assistant, now animated, replied, 'If I win, I certainly won't be working here any longer, I'll pack up this dreadful job immediately.'

Well, that conversation is really rather sad – as if the only way that the customer could look forward to getting the carpet in her living room changed was through the lottery, and how sad for the shop assistant to be going to work each day, doing a job he hated with his only hope of getting out being a win on the lottery.

PUT MONEY ON YOUR OWN SUCCESS

That was the downside. The good side is that people have something to look forward to that night by watching the lottery and they have those few hours of hope.

In this book, your hope will not be based upon a get-rich-quick success. Your hope will be based upon realities you can achieve.

The odds of your achieving your own success are better than you will ever be offered by any form of gambling because the odds for you are evens. The chance of a jackpot win on the lottery is approximately 16 million to 1, a win on a good horse might be 20 to 1, but the chance of your winning in your own life are evens. You can be successful or not – the choice really is yours.

Help others and help yourself

One of the amazing, yet fascinating, realities of successful people is that they rarely achieve success on their own. Success is usually achieved with the support, encouragement, enthusiasm, advice and help of others. It is equally true that the key to achieving what you want is to help enough people to get what they want first. It is then an absolute guaranteed certainty that you cannot fail to be successful.

In my book *Motivate to Win*, I discuss the qualities of great managers, and one type of great manager is the manager who takes enormous pride in the people who have been under his or her wing and who then move into other jobs, careers, vocations and achieve outstanding success.

A great manager understands that management is about helping people to grow, and I admit to the pleasure and pride I feel when other people tell me of their successes and achievements through a little help I may have given them at some stage.

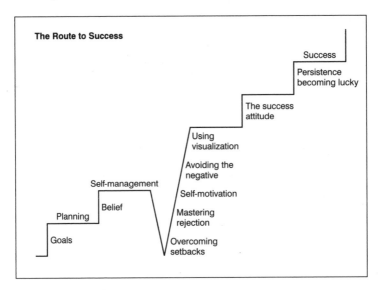

The Route to Success

Success

Persistence becoming lucky

The success attitude

Using visualization

Avoiding the negative

Self-management

Self-motivation

Belief

Planning

Mastering rejection

Goals

Overcoming setbacks

In order to achieve true success (maybe through financial independence, security, success in your profession or some outstanding sporting achievement), you must ensure that your ultimate goals will make you happy, or they will have little purpose. Throughout this book, when success is mentioned, it is intrinsically linked to happiness – success without happiness is not success.

You can be, and I believe you will be, a winner: successful, wealthy, loved and respected, by practising the philosophy and principles in *Succeed for Yourself*. Yes you can!

Pocket Reminders

- Define what success means for you
- Distinguish between success and money
- Start to believe in yourself
- Don't depend on the chance win – invest in yourself
- Look in the right direction for success
- Happiness is a result of your own efforts
- Consider the power of hope
- See how many other people you can make successful.

WISE WORDS

We have forty million reasons for failure, but not a single excuse.

Rudyard Kipling

2

Your Greatest Asset

Let me ask you, what do you consider to be your most valuable asset? Could it be your home, your car, your savings, or perhaps even your pension fund? The truth is, of course, that none of these is truly valuable.

YOUR MOST VALUABLE ASSET

Your most valuable asset is *you*: your mind. Everyone wants their assets and valuables to be secure. This chapter looks at how you can value and protect your most valuable asset.

I was brought up to believe that security was achieved through getting a good job with a big company. For three-quarters of the 20th century, this was basically true, but things are a little different these days. There are very few opportunities for a job for life now and many people realize that they cannot rely on current or future employment for their long-term security.

If we accept that we can no longer obtain security through a 'job for life', we can concentrate on effectively protecting our most valuable assets – ourselves. Surely then our lives will become more secure, safe and enjoyable. Common sense tells us that if we utilize our assets to their full potential, there will be a dramatic effect on our lives.

PREPARE FOR A JOURNEY

Imagine acquiring a new car. Prior to setting off on the first journey, it makes sense to be sure exactly what we are driving off in. We familiarize ourselves with the controls, get to know exactly where the indicators and the horn are. We test the strength of the brakes, we check and adjust the seat position and, crucially, check the oil, tyre pressure and how much fuel is in the tank. Now imagine this car is the little Mercedes Smart Car – could you take this car on a journey from London to Moscow? Of course you could, but you would have totally different preparation procedures from those needed when taking this car from London to Watford.

Use this analogy when embarking on the next journey of your life, so begin by taking stock and seeing exactly what is available to you.

AUDIT YOUR OWN PERSONAL ASSETS AND LIABILITIES

Every limited company, once a year, commissions its auditors to prepare statutory accounts, and within these accounts, assets and liabilities are clearly listed. I want you to carry out your own personal audit.

TANGIBLE ASSETS	
ASSETS	**LIABILITIES**
Home (value £x) Home contents (value £x) TV and audio-visual equipment Computer Premium Bonds, shares, ISAs, etc Building society savings Endowment Pension	Mortgage (£x per month) Car loan (£x per month) HP loans (£x per month) Overdraft (£x)

MY TANGIBLE ASSETS	
ASSETS	**LIABILITIES**

INTANGIBLE ASSETS	
ASSETS	**LIABILITIES**
Personal strengths/qualities Good team player, good rapport with subordinates & bosses, etc	*Personal weaknesses* Lack of self-confidence at times Not assertive enough
Skills/achievements/qualifications Degree, on-the-job qualifications, management experience, etc	Poor time management
Physical health/fitness Reasonably fit, rarely unwell	Overweight smoker
Friends/families support Close family network Single? Married? Divorced?	Single? Married? Divorced?

MY INTANGIBLE ASSETS	
ASSETS	**LIABILITIES**

First of all, create the tangible asset and liability statement. List on one side your current assets. These will include your home, car, possessions, investments, shares, etc. On the other side, list your liabilities: an overdraft or loan, unpaid bills or perhaps a hire purchase agreement. Use the examples on page 17 to create your own list of tangible assets/liabilities.

Now repeat the exercise, setting out your intangible asset and liability statement. On one side, list your personal strengths and qualities, skills and achievements, your qualifications, your experiences, physical health and fitness, how you think your friends, family and social contacts may feel about you and so on. On the other side, list your liabilities. These could be personal weaknesses such as fear of rejection, complacency, a tendency to procrastinate or a lack of self-discipline. Use the example to create your own list of intangible assets/liabilities.

You will see the importance of these two exercises when we come to Chapter 4 – Becoming Lucky. Like most people, you may well undervalue your most valuable asset: your mind. It is almost impossible to put a monetary figure on its worth – the courts have tried for years in insurance and damage claims. I read once of a person tragically brain-damaged for the remainder of her life. Her body was to continue to function and live a normal life span, but she would be unable to communicate and unable to reciprocate any feeling. She could be classified as brain dead. The individual received £4 million in compensation.

Would you sell your brain for £4 million, £10 million or £100 million? Of course not, but most of us totally undervalue the most incredible piece of equipment that we were born with. Your wealth, security, happiness and success will be very much dependent upon how you use *what you already have.*

SEARCHING FOR SUCCESS

I once heard the following story and it had such an impact on my thinking that I repeat it here. During the days of the South African diamond rush, a farmer heard about the enormous wealth to be gained from diamonds and in due course sold his farm to go searching. After a number of years without success, he became more disillusioned and desperate. One day, in complete despair, he threw himself off a bridge and drowned. It was just about that time that the person who had bought his farm happened to be walking through a dry river bed. He came across a rock of rather unusual shape and size. He took this rock to be analysed and found it to be a diamond of great value. It was shortly afterwards discovered that the farm was covered with similar rocks, and eventually it turned out to be one of the world's wealthiest diamond mines. Two powerful messages come out of this story. If only that farmer who had owned that land originally had taken the two steps necessary in order to achieve the wealth that he was seeking: first, learning what a diamond looked like in its natural state, and secondly, looking to what he already owned.

Preparing for a new challenge

Many people fail to prepare themselves for new challenges and opportunities for achieving wealth and happiness. Those who do achieve are continually learning, changing and developing, being trained and coached, seeking out new ideas. The fact that you are reading this book shows that you are one of these people who have the desire to progress.

Assess what you already have

The other message from the story above is to make more of what you already have. The grass is not always greener on the other side; the answer does not always lie somewhere else.

REMOVING YOUR LIABILITIES, ENHANCING YOUR ASSETS

Look back at your list of intangible liabilities. The items need not remain there permanently – that depends entirely on you because you have the most incredible equipment planted directly between your ears, which can do anything if it really wants to.

Your brain is more powerful than any computer that humankind will ever create. The greatest developments in the future are not going to be in the form of new technology, data processing, modes of travel or communication. They are going to come from increased use of the human brain.

Focusing on a desired result

Just a simple little example that I am sure you have experienced, perhaps even subconsciously. Before setting off on a journey, have you ever thought and really concentrated on where you want to park your car upon arrival at your destination? You visualize the potential spot and, sure enough, upon arrival it is vacant. I have experienced this countless times, to the extent that I now intentionally, and with forethought, choose a parking space before starting out on a journey. That space is invariably vacant.

HOW TO LOOK AFTER YOUR ASSETS

If the brain is so important, how should you look after it? Throughout this book I will be referring to the information you put into your brain and the expectations that you have of it (see especially Chapter 3 – Believe in Yourself). Although the brain is not a muscle, it does work like a muscle in some ways, in that the more it is used, the fitter it becomes and the better it performs.

First, the brain works better with healthier blood circulation. It requires oxygen from the blood system to be pumped through it. The amount of oxygen is increased through exercise. I have found that when I am taking exercise and my body is fitter, my brain becomes less stressed, it makes better decisions, is more able to cope and is more relaxed. It *responds* instead of simply reacting, and I generally feel better.

The more the brain is used, the stronger it becomes. Universities create the right conditions for minds to meet; where people can discuss and challenge each other's thoughts and research. In such an environment, the brain is nurtured.

Having the right qualifications

Many organizations, quite understandably, look for qualifications and academic achievement because these prove that the individual not only has a willingness to learn, but also has a powerful retention factor. This can provide an indication of someone's intelligence, but does not indicate common sense, attitude or an ability to communicate. Put all these together and you really do have a power to be reckoned with, a person highly sought-after by employers.

Exercise for the brain

Have you ever been in a brainstorming session where a few people get together to positively brainstorm a particular challenge or problem and nobody is allowed to say anything negative? It is amazing what can be achieved as people start to dig into their brain for creative ideas. It is always best to avoid making decisions in a brainstorming session, but to take them some 24 hours later.

I have found that after a long vacation, when I embark on my first speaking engagements the words never flow quite so well. Has it got anything to do with my vocal cords? Of course not; it is because my brain has not been used for a little while and it gets out of practice.

Logic and creativity

We all process information differently (as we will see in the chapter on communication), but our thought processes can be defined as falling roughly into two groups: left brain, giving rise to a convergent thinker for whom logic is paramount; and right brain, resulting in a divergent thinker for whom creativity is the more powerful influence.

To determine what type of thinking you use, please look at the five shapes overleaf and circle the one you instinctively find most attractive.

Shape 1

Shape 2

Shape 3

Shape 4

Shape 5

Shape 1

An extremely left-brain and logical thinker. This type of thinker is normally very methodical and utilizes logic for its own sake. As a rule, he or she is quite able and prepared to work alone.

Shape 2

This type of thinker is also very logical, although a little more flexible in his or her thinking, and prefers to work as part of a team.

Shape 3

Predominantly a logical thinker, but observe the shape. This person will use logic to make a decision, provided it takes them or their operation upwards and onwards. This person is always aiming to go forward.

Shape 4

A predominantly right-brain and creative thinker. Looking at the shape, you can see that this person keeps rolling along and bouncing back.

Shape 5

Predominantly an extremely right-brain and creative thinker. This person can be the master of the unexpected and a snappy or unconventional dresser.

The purpose of this exercise is really a little bit of fun and probably only tells you what you already know, but nevertheless, it will help you in establishing what sort of thinker you really are.

INVESTING IN YOURSELF

The body's prime function is to transport the brain. The majority of us spend vast amounts of money on the care and appearance of this transportation system, but it is quite extraordinary how mean we can be to the brain.

One of the best investments you can ever make is in yourself. Take yourself to a lecture or a seminar. Expose your brain to new thoughts, radical thinking and knowledge. Give your brain the opportunity to read. Let your brain learn from videos and CDs. The small cost is an investment from which you and your family can reap untold rewards.

It is great to see so many people buying more and more books on cookery, sports, fitness and other hobbies. The investment that you make in a self-help or personal development book can bring untold rewards of success in the future. Feed your brain with knowledge – it has a great thirst for usable information. Most people spend a great deal of time travelling in cars, buses, trains or aeroplanes – time which is usually wasted. So, turn your car into a learning centre and put a CD into your personal stereo. Listen to business and educational learning cassettes or CDs. Change this wasted time to productive and achievement time. The extraordinary thing about playing personal development CDs is that you are continually hearing something new. Many of those I carry with me I have listened to 30 or 40 times over the years, and I cannot recall an occasion when I have not heard something new. The words themselves have never changed, but as my experiences, mood and thoughts change, so does the information I draw from them.

Your brain is your greatest asset; you own the equipment, the winning lottery ticket, the black box of achievement, and you have the certainty and the security that you can do and achieve anything you want to!

I finish this chapter by repeating that you have the equipment for success and happiness. The greater part of this book is devoted to showing you how to use this asset (equipment) so that it will deliver to you your hopes and dreams. It is your responsibility, and I mean *your* responsibility, to value and take care of this incredible tool, just as the master craftsman, craftswoman, chef or golfer takes care of their equipment.

Pocket Reminders

- Consider your most valuable asset – yourself
- Audit your *tangible* assets and liabilities
- Audit your *intangible* assets and liabilities
- Prepare for a new challenge
- Look after your assets
- Keep your brain in good shape: take regular exercise
- Invest in yourself: listen to CDs and read books that develop the mind.

WISE WORDS

If we did all the things we were capable of, we would literally astound ourselves.

Thomas A Edison

3

Believe in Yourself

Let me ask you a question: how do you see yourself ? Or, to put it another way, what is your self-image?

No doubt you can respond quite quickly, but now spend a little bit of time really thinking about yourself. Not about what others may think of you, because they may have completely the wrong impression, but how you actually see yourself.

Some people, as they achieve success in life, build their ego and then have an insatiable appetite to feed this ego. It is important for us all to have an ego, but not an ego problem. There is a saying: the bigger the ego, the smaller the bank balance. I remember an Australian saying to me many years ago, 'Be nice to people on the way up, because you meet the same ones on the way back down again.' It is very useful advice. Looking at my own experiences to date, I have had some amazing highs and some equally incredible lows, and that little message has stood me in good stead.

SELF-IMAGE

Your self-image is the key to your success. You will perform exactly as you see yourself, so your opinion of yourself is extremely important if you are aiming for success. We have all heard the expression 'Some people are their own worst enemy.' It is true; they really are. Sometimes people experience an inferiority complex and, if we're honest, we have all experienced that at some stage in our lives or in certain situations. Poor self-image is a more fundamental problem than the occasional feeling of inferiority. A person with a poor self-image communicates their negativity in their dealings with others.

No doubt you have seen, or perhaps currently have, friends who are under pressure: marital problems, stress at work, redundancy, depression and, of course, poor self-image. These things are apparent in how they look and in what they say. Their appearance is not cared for: less attention is paid to hair, make-up, cleanliness and body odour. Some people overeat and become obese. It can affect their posture and the way they walk. They may even avoid people and become withdrawn.

Some of the problems I have described above are things that can honestly and justifiably be explained as 'outside the individual's control'. There are events that happen and are sometimes outside our immediate control, but there are also self-inflicted, avoidable pressures.

Perpetuating a poor self-image

It is important to understand that poor self-image is usually self-perpetuating. Our behaviour tends to be repetitive, the continual replaying of old patterns. The cure is simple: you must change the way you see yourself.

Most people are unaware of or choose not to accept the need to change. Some, quite extraordinarily, appear to gain some weird kind of satisfaction by wallowing in their own self-pity and this, to a certain extent, becomes security for them. Success and achievement frighten them because they spend so much of their time thinking about their situation that to break out of the pattern becomes too hard to do and their confidence and self-image plummet even further.

BUILDING YOUR SELF-CONFIDENCE

Mostly, confidence is talked about from a negative view-point, with people focusing on their lack of self-confidence rather than finding ways to build it.

A little while ago my company created a video called: *How to Build Your Confidence*. This video, among others, was supplied to one of the great British banks, HSBC, and went into its library. Of some 500 books, videos and audio cassettes, it became the most used and popular item. The library was open for free use to every member of the bank's staff.

Naturally, we were all interested to find out why it was so popular and our research showed that very few people will actually voice to anyone else, let alone their immediate superior, their concern about their lack of confidence. But given the chance to find a solution privately through a library, they will try to improve their confidence level. This research indicates that many people would like to develop their levels of self-confidence. Many people believe that confidence is one of the bases for success, achievement, strong self-image and earning the respect of others.

We all experience a lack of confidence from time to time, particularly when we are doing something new. Confidence comes from the continual repetition of certain activities.

You no doubt have heard people say, 'I have had 15 years' experience.' This in many cases can be one year's experience repeated 15 times, but nevertheless, confidence will have grown with the passing of years and the repetition of the experiences.

Take for example a uniformed policeman patrolling the streets each day. After a period of time he would become extremely confident. But ask him to make a speech to 2,000 people at the Wembley Conference Centre and he would, of course, experience a loss of confidence the moment he received the invitation.

WHAT GOES INTO YOUR BRAIN?

In Chapter 2, we talked about our brain being our greatest asset. For the purpose of this example, I would now like to describe it in its purest and simplest form as being like a box.

– Negative input
What people say about me.
What I think about myself.

+ Positive input
What people say about me.
What I say about myself.

Into that box are placed experiences and information that are both negative and positive.

Obviously some experiences and information will not fall into either category. It could be information that we have gained, but which we may not yet have any particular use for. I would put such information on the positive side.

Let me give you some examples of what I mean. Some of the positive things people might say to you:

- 'You're looking fantastic!'
- 'You're looking really well.'
- 'You've done that job superbly.'
- 'Could you do this, as you're the best person to do it?'
- 'Thank you, that was a wonderful result.'
- 'I know if you do it, it will get a positive result.'
- 'You do it, because you're better than me.'
- 'I can rely on you.'

Then there is also the information that we put in ourselves:

- 'I'm feeling great.'
- 'I feel well.'
- 'I can do it.'
- 'I really enjoy this.'
- 'I know I am going to like you.'
- 'Today is going to be a great day.'
- 'I've got a great brain.'
- 'I can solve it.'

Now consider some of the negative things people might say to you:

- 'You look terrible.'
- 'You really messed that up.'
- 'No, not you, you're not the right person.'
- 'I knew you wouldn't do it properly.'
- 'You are just not going to make it.'
- 'No, not you, you're not experienced enough.'
- 'You're completely useless.'
- 'I can't rely on you.'

These are the negative things that you might say to yourself:

- 'I'm feeling terrible.'
- 'I feel ill.'
- 'I can't.'
- 'I hate doing this job.'
- 'I know I'm not going to like that person.'
- 'Today is going to be one of those days.'

- 'I bet there will be nowhere to park the car.'
- 'I'm sure I've got something seriously wrong with me.'
- 'I'm just not clever enough.'
- 'I don't have what it takes.'
- 'Anyhow, I'm never lucky.'

The brain stores this information, so we can see how important it is to control what we allow to go in and what we put in ourselves, because, as with a computer, if you put rubbish in, you get rubbish out.

```
–  –  –  –  –  –        +  +  +  +  +  +
–  –  –  –  –  –        +  +  +  +  +  +
–  –  –  –  –  –        +  +  +  +  +  +
–  –  –  –  –  –        +  +  +  +  +  +
–  –  –  –  –  –        +  +  +  +  +  +
–  –  –  –  –  –        +  +  +  +  +  +
–  –  –  –  –  –        +  +  +  +  +  +
```

What is your brain filled with?

Be careful from now on what you allow people to put into your brain and, much more importantly, what it is that you are putting in yourself.

HOW WE ARE CONDITIONED

We have all been conditioned by our life experiences, so our reactions, thoughts, feelings, emotions, image, confidence and so on are mainly developed through three forms of conditioning: our childhood, our environment and how we deal with past experiences. However, the fact that we have been conditioned is not a reason to accept where we are, nor is it an excuse for us not to try to change; and it is most certainly not a basis upon which you can say, 'Well, that rules me out from achieving what I want.' If you understand and use your past conditioning positively, dealing with it can be one of those stages on your success map.

Childhood

First of all, we are conditioned by our childhood. Every child is born with a positive brain. In the early weeks and months of any baby's life, parents are very supportive, motivational and encouraging. They are always smiling at their newborns, as are visitors and family friends. In the past, it was believed that babies were born with impaired eyesight; this, we now know, is not strictly true. There is evidence that babies can even see when inside their mother's womb. After a few weeks of life seeing parents' and visitors' faces all smiling at them, they respond with a smile. The first one or two may be of a windy sort, but then the real smiles come through.

Parents now continually inject confidence and belief into their children by means of statements like 'You *can* crawl', 'You *can* speak', 'You *can* walk'. This is all positive conditioning.

The day their child is fully mobile is often the day the positive conditioning ceases. It is no longer 'You can do it.' It is 'You can't', 'You shouldn't', 'Don't touch', 'Come here!'

Many children, throughout their childhood years, experience poor-quality teachers who do not motivate or encourage them. Some parents or teachers even say to children, 'You're useless', 'You're stupid', 'You'll never be a success', continually dwelling on the negative. At the height of the recession in the early 1990s, some teachers warned school leavers that they would never get a job in their lives, and prepared them for a life on the dole. By the end of the decade, there was virtually full employment.

Our childhood experiences naturally condition our brain and affect the way we respond and react to future situations.

Environment – who we mix with

The second form of conditioning is a form of environmental conditioning. Whatever environment you are in, over a period of time you are likely to conform to it. It is said that if you only mix with millionaires, it is virtually impossible not to become one. We have all heard parents say, 'Don't let that child get into bad company.' Why? Because a child from a safe and secure, well-behaved family who chooses to mix with hoodlums will almost certainly become one. The Jesuits believe that a person's life is formed during their first seven years.

As adults, we are consciously and subconsciously conditioned by our environment. Have you noticed that football managers seem to wear the same sort of clothes and all chew gum and move their heads in a particular way when they are being interviewed? Can you tell the difference between people who work in the public sector and those who work in the private sector? You will have experienced totally different behaviour from family, friends, colleagues and yourself as you move in different environments.

Environmental conditioning permeates every part of society and affects every one of us both positively and negatively. We naturally try to conform to the environment in which we are operating. At one extreme, people will change their appearance and even spend vast sums of money to fit into a particular environment. Ladies' Day at Royal Ascot is an example. The hats worn on that day almost certainly will never be worn again – you would hardly wear that sort of hat to go shopping in the middle of winter.

We are all born to be positive and conditioned to be negative. The world in which we live creates a negative effect which hampers positive success.

Naturally we try to conform. In the business world it is very interesting, though sad, to see a salesperson going through a bad spell seeking out the company of others who are also doing badly. There are others, however, who are more positive and do the opposite. In a tough situation, experiencing loss of confidence and lack of sales, they will mix only with the superstars. If you mix with people who are positive, cheerful, enthusiastic and expecting the best – even though perhaps you may not be feeling too positive – it is absolutely certain that within a short period of time, by being in that company you will become more positive and cheerful.

For those of my readers who are parents, be aware that there has been continual erosion of correct pronunciation and use of the English language within schools and the communities that our young people mix in. It is, and always will be, a prerequisite for people hoping to advance in their careers, maximize their potential or be given the responsibility of leadership to be able to speak well with the right pronunciation and with a greater command of their language. Help your young people achieve this ability.

Past experiences

The third form of conditioning is conditioning by past experience.

Success experience   Failure experience
↓   ↓
Confidence   Lack of confidence
↓   ↓
I can do it   I can't or I'm no
                                 good at that

An experience of success registered in your brain builds your confidence and results in a subconscious confidence that 'I can do that'. All the best coaches, trainers and personal developers try to give people success experiences.

On the other hand, a failure experience can create a lack of confidence and a subconscious response that 'I can't do that' or 'I'm no good at that'. The more you think 'I can't' or 'I'm no good', the more those negatives will destroy those positive brain cells.

Despite all this, the past is not an excuse, nor is it a justification for anything in the future. Let the past be as it should be: a part of history with experiences that can be used positively.

I recall my first visit to South Africa, shortly after that most incredible election when Nelson Mandela exhibited to the world one of the greatest and what must surely be the most admired human qualities. Many years of his life were spent in prison, but at no time after his release or after he was elected president did he hold any bitterness against his captors or those who imprisoned him. He spent little time when making speeches looking backwards: everything was about the future. Looking to the future was not a reaction to some bitterness or to some aspect of his years of struggle, but came from a determination to achieve a greater freedom and empowerment for the black people of South Africa.

It is desperate to see the reverse in other nations. Fears and bitterness from the past become the barriers to a wonderful future.

HOW TO BUILD YOUR SELF-IMAGE

Let us now move forward and look at how we can build and maintain a healthy self-image, which in turn builds self-confidence.

1. No more excuses

Never make an excuse to try to justify your failure to achieve your goals, ambitions and success. They are what they are: excuses, not justifications. Here is a list of some of the more common excuses:

- 'I'm never in the right place at the right time.'
- 'I'm just not lucky.'
- 'I'm too young.'
- 'I'm not made that way.'
- 'It's my parents' fault.'
- 'I didn't go to the right school.'
- 'If only I had been to university.'
- 'If only I were healthier.'
- 'I was just born under the wrong birth sign.'

So promise yourself: 'I will make no more excuses.'

2. Have pride in yourself

Take another look at those intangible assets that you wrote down earlier in this chapter. This is who you are and what you have to offer. Just look at the physical and mental attributes you have. Have faith and belief in yourself, and give your brain a chance to perform. You are good and you are going to get better.

3. Take care of your appearance

Have you really looked in the mirror lately – and I don't mean a superficial check-over? Do you really look successful? Is your appearance giving the image of the person you would like to be? If the outside looks good, it will really help you to feel good inside. How often have we heard people say, 'I feel so much better' after having their hair restyled or buying some new clothes – they even seem to have a greater air of self-confidence.

Have you ever stood outside a hairdresser's and watched people come out: their body language, movements, their glances in shop windows as they make their way home; there is always a greater confidence, pride and enhanced self-image. The money you spend on your appearance is worthwhile, but do not go to the extreme. The ultimate extreme is the person whose ego drives them to be continually spending ridiculous sums unnecessarily – hence the phrase 'The bigger the ego, the smaller the bank balance.' So try not to become self-obsessed.

4. Check what you allow into your brain

Imagine a filter or a sieve that prevents certain unpleasant thoughts getting through. Do not allow other people to sabotage your assets or your success and, equally, do not do it yourself. If you catch yourself in self-destruct mode, say to yourself, 'I'm not going to think that', and replace that negative thought with a positive one, just as you would go through a punnet of strawberries picking out bad ones – discard the rotten thoughts. It takes a little bit of practice and, in some cases, courage and determination, not to think negatively.

5. Believe you can

Belief is a powerful word. It is used predominantly within a religious context. As I respect all true believers, I do not consider that I have the right to say that one religion is right and another is wrong. People throughout history have followed others with belief and conviction.

Linford Christie became the 100-metre Olympic champion at 34 years of age. Did he have a better body than the other athletes? Or was he younger than the other athletes? No. He achieved Olympic and world success by overcoming the opinions of highly intelligent 'experts' who said he was too old; they believed that, past the age of 24, the body was incapable of running at that speed. But Linford Christie believed he could.

One of my own passions is horse riding. All instructors, when teaching riders to jump fences, say you must throw your *heart* over first, because if you believe you can, your horse will pick up that message. By believing this, the rider will sit better and jump better. If you *believe* you can, the result is almost certain success. Believe you cannot, start to hestitate and the horse will almost certainly hestitate, put its front brakes on, dig its toes in and the jockey will have to try to defy gravity.

6. Make positive statements

Speak positively. What we normally do is the reverse. For example, if you say, 'I'm not feeling very confident', what happens? You get exactly that result. Another example is 'I'm not feeling very well' – say that, and you will feel that way as a result. So reverse the messages from the negative to the positive and you will be giving positive instructions to your brain.

Every personal development teacher, trainer or coach always stresses the importance of making positive affirmations. These powerful statements create tremendous impact on the subconscious, and it is even more effective when these positive statements are said just before going to sleep and then are repeated first thing in the morning. Examples of such positive affirmations include:

- 'I am confident.'
- 'I am feeling great.'

- 'I am a good speaker.'
- 'I am successful.'
- 'I am financially secure.'
- 'I am feeling well.'
- 'I am ....' [fill in your positive affirmation here]
- 'I am ....' [fill in your positive affirmation here]
- 'I am ....' [fill in your positive affirmation here]
- 'I am ....' [fill in your positive affirmation here]
- 'I am ....' [fill in your positive affirmation here]
- 'I am ....' [fill in your positive affirmation here]

Do not ever make the mistake of saying, 'I am *going* to be...' This is stored in the subconscious and only puts a dampener on your positive thoughts. Allow your subconscious mind to clearly focus on the desired *result* and that result will become inevitable.

7. Do not fear mistakes

It is impossible to make a mistake if you do absolutely nothing, but of course if you do absolutely nothing, you achieve absolutely nothing as well.

Mistakes, errors or what some people might even term failures are, of course, only 'unsatisfactory results'. Every mistake is an experience from which you can gain information and, if you are sensible, can help build a successful future.

It is very easy for executives to get into the 'no-decision syndrome': the trap of being so fearful of making an error that they actually fail to make any decisions. All the greatest success stories have involved some mistakes. Some entrepreneurs actually claim that they have made more mistakes and errors than good decisions, but that the successful decisions have greatly outweighed the errors.

8. Do some charitable work

Let's go back to one of the original principles: that it is impossible not to be successful if you are helping other people to get what they want. If only every unemployed person would spend a little of their time in charitable work, particularly helping others less fortunate, they would automatically do themselves a dramatic favour in building their self-esteem, confidence, image and belief, and that alone would help them towards their own employment prospects.

Try to devote a little time towards helping others, even though you may be extremely busy or already highly successful. That little bit of time spent will help build your own self-belief, image and confidence.

9. Check your environment

If you are continually mixing with people who destroy your confidence, are very negative or maybe cynical and disparaging about success and achievement, move out of that environment and try to mix with people who are positive, enthusiastic and who are 'builders' rather than 'takers'. Mixing with people who are success-orientated will again make it virtually impossible for you not to be successful.

10. Compile a 'success record'

Go back to your earliest memory of success – perhaps when you were at school – and from that earliest memory, compile a record of every successful experience you have had, in both your business and your personal life. This information can be stored in a scrapbook with photographs, letters and cuttings. Apart from anything else, it is very enjoyable to do and interesting for your family, but most importantly of all, in times of self-doubt or even loss of confidence, this record will help to re-establish your shaken self-belief.

Pocket Reminders

- Consider your own self-image
- Have pride in yourself and build your self-confidence
- Check what you allow into your brain – try to eliminate negative inputs
- Consider your conditioning, but do not allow it to be an excuse for being negative.

Ten steps to building your self-image:

1. Do not make excuses for not achieving your goals

2. Have pride in yourself

3. Take care of your appearance (ensure you have the right image)

4. Check what you allow into your brain (filter out unpleasant thoughts)

5. Believe you can

6. Make positive statements

7. Do not fear mistakes

8. Do some charitable work

9. Check your environment (ensure you mix with positive people)

10. Compile a 'success record'.

WISE WORDS

If you only look at what it is, you might never attain what it could be.

Bits and Pieces

We have been taught to believe that negative equals realistic and positive equals unrealistic.

Susan Jeffers

4

Becoming Lucky

If only I could parcel up some luck and sell it in packages – what a potential market: millions upon millions of sure-fire customers just waiting to get rid of their money into my bank account.

THE LUCK 'BUSINESS'

Selling and marketing 'luck' has been big business since time immemorial. From witch doctors to way-out religious cults, from clairvoyants to 'get rich quick' conmen, all have prospered at the expense of the weak or the vulnerable. We all know you cannot buy luck, but we still hanker after it.

These are a few of the ideas that I have heard of and tried, but which have not worked:

- I have thrown money into a pool of water apparently called a wishing well – the only person who seems to gain luck is the owner of the pool.
- I have thrown salt over my shoulder when I have spilt it on the table.

- I have turned my silver coin in front of a new moon.
- I have kissed the Blarney stone.
- I have tried never to break a mirror.
- I do not walk under ladders.
- I do not walk on the lines on a pavement.
- I always pull the wishbone.
- I say 'white rabbits' on the first of every month.
- I make a wish every time I cut a birthday cake.
- I cross my fingers.
- I never look at a full moon through glass.
- I don't put a hat on in bed.

However, in my experience, no superstitions designed to attract luck work. Moreover, superstitions in one country can be completely reversed in another.

Even if you do not see yourself as superstitious, I bet you have said one of the following:

- 'I had a bit of luck.'
- 'I was very lucky.'
- 'Well, it was just a bit of luck.'

Or perhaps:

- 'I never have any luck.'
- 'I'm not a lucky sort of person.'

Of course you have – and so have I!

DISTINGUISH BETWEEN LUCK AND CHANCE

The truth is that luck is available for you; maybe not in the way that you wish, but you can become lucky. Let us start to put this into some sort of perspective. No doubt you have seen or listened to an interview with a successful actress or actor, singer or model. They nearly always say, 'Well, I was lucky' or 'I just had a little bit of luck'. Surely what they are really saying is 'I made an effort, got off my backside and got myself into the right place at the right time.'

It seems that every successful person always claims that he or she had a bit of luck. May I suggest that this is modesty. It is also interesting that people who classify themselves as unsuccessful attribute their lack of success to *bad* luck. We must therefore understand and distinguish between luck and chance, as there really is a very big difference.

Chance

Chance can be a win on the horses, the lottery, the football pools or a throw of the dice. Chance is something that is totally out of your control, so to base your life, hopes, prosperity or success on it is a soul-destroying approach that will only breed dissatisfaction.

Betting shops are full of people trying to be lucky. If they invested the money and time they spend selecting the so-called winning horse in themselves, can you imagine what they could achieve for themselves and their family?

What would you do if you won £8 million on the lottery? I was asked this question and I found myself saying that I would do exactly what I am doing now. I would change very little. I can assure you, however, that I will never be dependent upon a chance win to provide my life's happiness when it is so much easier, faster and downright certain when you invest in yourself.

THE 'LUCK PRINCIPLE'

The simplest and most direct explanation of luck I have come across is as follows:

L	Labour
U	Under
C	Correct
K	Knowledge

Labour

The first word may not appear to be highly motivational because it implies work, but what it really means is 'do something'.

At one of the conferences I was speaking at we needed to get the attendees to be more proactive. I asked everybody to stand up and then said to the delegates, 'Now lift up your chair and look under the seat. If you find anything, hold it high in a raised hand.' You can imagine the noise as 2,000 people got off their chairs to look, and then the shouts of excitement, because pinned underneath some 20 chairs was a £5 note. The message I conveyed was that if you want to make money, get off your backside.

Correct knowledge

So, what is correct knowledge? Correct knowledge is:

- knowing where you are today;
- knowing where you want to be or go; and
- having a plan.

The first stage in establishing correct knowledge is to make a completely honest assessment of where you are today. You will already have audited your own personal assets and liabilities in Chapter 2 – Your Greatest Asset. You will have listed your strengths, weaknesses, assets, experiences, knowledge and contacts, and generally considered what you have to offer. So, to know where you are today is to have a sense of pride in yourself that corresponds with reality.

The second stage is knowing where you want to go. We have all heard the cliché 'A person going nowhere normally gets there.' In Chapter 7 – Goals, I will look specifically at how to set your goals and how to decide what those goals should be; how to have purpose, how to always have something to look forward to.

You must have goals. There is not one successful person in the history of humankind who has not achieved their success by consciously or subconsciously having purpose and goals. So, for you to be lucky, goals are essential. If you omit goals from your action plan you will be dependent on chance.

The third and final stage of correct knowledge is having a plan to achieve these goals. This will be covered in Chapter 8 – Personal Planning.

Again, let me remind you that every achievement has come through visualizing goals and by carrying out a systematic plan to achieve these goals. So, if you really do want to use the 'luck principle', remember you do not become lucky by sitting on your backside waiting for the phone to ring, for the postman to arrive or for the right numbers to come up on the lottery!

While preparing this chapter, I had a telephone call from one of the United Kingdom's most successful training managers, Samantha Allen. I enquired as to how well her husband was doing in his new business venture (also as a trainer). Sam's reply was 'Rick is really busy; he's had a lot of luck and the work keeps rolling in. We're just worried that the luck may run out.'

Sam's reply exemplifies everything I have said so far about luck. Had Rick been lucky? Yes, because he had *made* himself lucky. My reply to Sam was 'If Rick keeps doing what he is currently doing, the luck will stay with him.' There is a saying that goes 'There are those that make things happen, those that watch things happen and there are those that wonder what happened.'

We have all heard interviews with famous entertainers, and isn't it fascinating how when they recall some of the events that turned their careers, their words are often prefaced with 'Well, I had a little bit of luck'? One of the most successful pop groups in the 1990s was the Spice Girls, but if you investigate their careers and the work and preparation, the commitment, the dedication and the hard times that they went through prior to their international acclaim, it becomes apparent that there was no luck involved. One of the greatest golfers of all time, Arnold Palmer, was quoted as saying, 'The harder I work, the luckier I get.'

Base your monetary future on luck (as we have defined it in this chapter) and you will become as lucky as you want to be. Amazingly, it works!

Luck is where planning meets opportunity – become lucky!

Pocket Reminders

Becoming lucky:

- Distinguish between luck and chance
- Use the 'luck principle'
- Know where you are today
- Know where you want to be or go
- Have a plan to get where you want to be.

WISE WORDS

I am a great believer in luck and I find the harder I work the more I have of it.

Stephen Leacock

5

Time: Your Greatest Resource

Every successful businessperson, when planning for the future, takes stock of business assets and available resources. You have already looked at your assets and, in particular, the greatest asset of all – your brain. I trust that by now you believe in yourself, your greatest asset, and that you have faith in what that asset will do for you.

So now let us concentrate on resources and on the greatest resource of all. This is a bank account that we all have in common, but a bank account with peculiarities: you cannot invest into this account, make a deposit or obtain a statement – all you can do is withdraw. It is the bank account of *time*. Every day, we take another day out of this bank account, yet this valuable resource cannot be replaced. It is tragic that so many people take their time for granted and undervalue each day. It only takes a visit to a hospice to spend time with people who are terminally ill to truly understand the value of time and of using it well.

WORK, REST AND PLAY

If we are really fortunate, our time is divided in three ways: a third of our life at work; a third at play (evenings, weekends, holidays and retirement); and a third asleep.

Work time and play time

If people are happy at work, they are generally more happy at play and vice versa. I believe that if people are unhappy in their private lives it can affect their performance and, of course, success at work.

As I understand it, the primary reason for going to work is to earn some money. Why do we want the money? To pay for our play time. I recall saying this on one of my courses, when Angela Heylin, the Chief Executive Director of the public relations company Charles Barker plc, said, 'I must disagree with that – I love my job.' I did not contradict, but shared that interesting thought with the rest of the audience. One member came back with a question: 'Angela, would you still go to work if you weren't being paid?' You can imagine the reply.

Of course, it is quite true that we go to work for lots of reasons, and the greatest motivator in the world for all of us is to do something we enjoy. If we can achieve this during work time, fantastic.

STRESS

The last few years has seen stress become a major concern in the business arena. More and more courses on how to manage stress are appearing. Thousands of corporations employ stress consultants. Vast sums of money are being expended on learning how to cope with stress, stress counselling and dealing with the results of stress. But it seems that very little effort or thought is being directed at the cause or the prevention.

My personal opinion is that stress is good, as long as it is managed. Stress, in some cases, results in better performance. Adrenalin can raise levels of achievement, but stress must be managed and prevented from causing a medical condition, which can be extremely serious. Doctors' surgeries are full of people suffering from stress, unhappiness, pressure and relationship problems.

Stress is not unique to the business world – it is found throughout the whole population. Years ago, when families were more united and living in closer proximity, these pressures could often be managed and problems solved within the family unit. Unfortunately, with the movement of population and the breaking up of families, many people are very lonely and do not have the security of a family unit to help them through times of strife and unhappiness. When we cannot see a way forward, our bodies become more vulnerable to illness.

The causes of stress

The biggest cause of stress at work is the mismanagement of time: people taking bulging briefcases home, not opening them, taking the same briefcase back to work and then feeling guilty. Piles of paperwork build up without action or decisions being taken.

The second biggest cause of stress is very simple: lack of training, or the 'square peg in a round hole' scenario. People who are put into jobs for which they have not been trained, or for which they are not qualified, become unable to cope. They then experience dramatic loss of confidence and feel terribly stressed due to the expectations of others and their inability to live up to the expectations of others – and still they receive no training.

Many people get promoted because they demonstrate skills or perform well in another arena and are then expected to be able to manage, lead and motivate, without being trained in how to do so.

The third cause of stress is sheer work overload with appraisal only once a year. Of course, another great source of stress, which has become more and more common, is the threat of redundancy.

Preventing stress

In the vast majority of cases, stress can so easily be prevented by training and by individuals personally developing themselves. But we still live in an environment where the majority of people spend very little money or time on their own personal development, and if their employers do not provide facilities or they are not available elsewhere, they never get the opportunity.

Although stress can be a useful motivator, it requires management through the effective use of time, learning, personal development and prioritizing.

ACTIVITY AND ACHIEVEMENT

There is a great difference between activity and achievement. Think of a time when you were busy all day but felt that you hadn't actually achieved anything, despite feeling as if you hadn't stopped. I suggest that when you go home you do not feel as good, as positive or even as relaxed – it has been 'one of those days'.

Now think of another day when you have also been busy, but it has been a day of achievement. You did that awful job you had been putting off for a while, you finished that report, you won some new business and it was a real day of progress and achievement. How did you feel that evening? Of course it will be a much more enjoyable evening and your play time will be more fulfilling.

So, how can you make every day a day of achievement rather than a day of activity? The very simple concept of time management has never really been improved upon, yet a whole industry grew out of the original idea: Filofaxes, personal organizers, palmtops, and numerous time management systems and planners. Many of them have complicated the simplicity of the original idea, but nevertheless will be very effective for you.

MANAGING YOUR TIME TO ACHIEVE MORE

Ivy Lee, an efficiency expert, was granted an interview by the president of a medium-sized steel company, Charles Schwab. Lee was in the process of explaining to the president how his firm's services could help him to manage his company better, when Schwab stated, 'We know what we should be doing now; if you can show me a way of getting more done in the same time available, I'll listen to you and pay you whatever you think it's worth.' Lee said, 'Fine, I'll give you a system; it will only take a few minutes to explain it to you. I would like you to use this idea, get your people to use this idea and you send me a cheque for whatever you think it's worth.'

Six weeks later, Lee received a cheque for $25,000 with a note attached to it that said from a monetary viewpoint, this was the finest lesson Schwab had ever learnt. Five years later, Schwab had taken that company to be the largest independent steel corporation in the world, the Bethlehem Steel Company, and he is now recognized and held in high esteem as being one of the greatest industrialists and managers in US history.

A simple time-management system

We all have the same 24 hours in every day, which breaks down to 86,400 seconds. The busiest people in the world – prime ministers and presidents, entrepreneurs, athletes, entertainers and business leaders – still have only 86,400 seconds in their day. They may have less play time than achievement time – in other words, they work longer hours – but they still have the same hours in the day as you and I.

If you really want to get more done in a day, try using the following system.

First, at the end of a day, just before you leave the office or finish your work for the day, draw up a list of the most important jobs to do the next day. This list can be in a diary, or even on a sheet of paper. It does not really matter what you call it – 'to do list' or the 'today list' – just do it at the end of the day. Secondly, number that list of tasks in their order of importance. Finally, the following day when you decide to start work, start at number one and keep on until it is complete and then progress to number two, and so on until you have worked your way through the list.

So why is the above system so effective? Let us see.

Making the system work

1. Compile lists the night before

This is the reverse of what so many of us used to do, ie prepare our plan for the day first thing in the morning. The problem with that was that while you were deciding on the activities for the day, the phone would ring, e-mails would arrive and people would come in with their own priorities, and before you knew it, the day would be out of control and you became reactive rather than proactive. Also, the brain is most effective in the early part of the day, so why waste energy making up your mind what to do, when you could be getting on and doing it? On my management courses, I always stress to managers the importance of delegating the night before, not first thing in the morning.

2. During the day, tick off the items

Ticking off completed tasks is highly motivational as you can see yourself progressing. So you will be managing your greatest asset, your brain, and be helping it to be more motivated and to perform more effectively.

3. Adhere to your list

Most days the list will not be completed, but if you adhere to it, the tasks that you concentrate on and complete will be the most important.

4. Prioritize and do the nasty job first

The number one of most lists is nearly always the most unpleasant. There is the temptation to do the quick and easy tasks first and then get round to the longer or more unpleasant jobs. You cannot kid yourself: if you know you have to do a rotten job, but you do the quick and easy ones instead, you never do them as well, as effectively or even as speedily because you know that rotten job is lurking in the background. On the other hand, when you have completed a rotten job, how do you feel? Relieved, elated and more motivated. Manage your assets and resources – it is amazing what can be achieved.

5. Deal with interruptions effectively

Finally, be realistic. Do you ever have a day when you can crack on with your list without interruption? I do not think I have ever had one. So how do you handle the interruptions, the phone calls, the emergency, the crisis or somebody else's demands? I have found the following to be most effective. Ask yourself: Is this more important than what I am doing now, yes or no? If it is more important, deal with it immediately, and if it is not, add it to the list somewhere.

You may be thinking: Well, that's all very well, but how do I make that decision?

Let me pass on a system of prioritization that I have found to be very effective in business. The number one priority is anything that earns revenue. It might be handling a customer complaint, it might be the dispatch, it might be the chance of an extra sale or business, but the number one priority must be revenue coming in. With that as a priority, yours and everybody else's future is more secure.

The second priority when faced with an interruption is helping somebody else. It may be a decision that has to be made, it may be some guidance or training or support. It may be a response to a memo or correspondence.

The third priority is dealing with problems, and it is very interesting that if the first two are operational, there are fewer of number three.

If we were in conversation you might say to me, 'Richard, do you really do your list every single day of your life?' And to be truthful, I have to admit that I do not, because there are some days when it is just not practical, but I can tell you that on the days that I do it exactly as I have explained, it is amazing how much actually gets done and how much more motivated I feel.

RELAXATION AND PLAY TIME

So, having managed your work time, it is just as important to make sure that the play time is really switching-off time. Many people do have difficulty switching off, and if you are one of those who has difficulty leaving your work behind, this may help. Imagine in your mind's eye a massive switch, and at 5.30 pm on a Friday just turn the switch off. On Monday morning at 8.00 am, turn the switch back on again. You just choose the times.

Saving time

Try handling a piece of paper only once. Pick it up and action it. A further thought to challenge you with: 'How much do you actually get through on the two days before you go away on holiday?' Fascinating, isn't it, how much we really do action, tidy up and complete – you could do that every day.

Procrastination

Procrastination (ie putting off things that need to be done) has to be beaten if you are going to achieve success. A procrastinator might say:

- 'Now is not the right time.'
- 'I'll get around to it.'
- 'The conditions aren't perfect at the moment.'

Do you imagine that successful people allow themselves to procrastinate? Of course not, but it is an absolute guaranteed characteristic of the non-achievers, or those who are dissatisfied.

Try using three little words that can be a powerful self-motivator: DO IT NOW. For many years, I carried them on the sun visor in my car, and I also put a tent card on my desk saying:

What am I doing now to get a sale?

This was a great self-motivator, and the guilt on seeing those words and doing nothing motivated me into immediate action.

Prime task time

There are certain times of the day that can become what I call 'prime task time'. For salespeople this is the most opportune time to be talking to customers and potential customers. So it is inefficient to use this time to write reports, prepare quotes or for any task other than talking to decision makers. These other jobs can be done outside prime selling time. Whatever your job or occupation, work out your prime task time and during that time only work on those tasks – you will be surprised at how much more you achieve.

Thinking time

It has long been recognized that achievers must have some thinking time. Many people do not allow themselves this special time and some even consider it to be a luxury. It is not a luxury – it is an essential for achievement. Most of us only allocate thinking time when we are in a car, driving, rather than perhaps allowing ourselves half a day a week, or even a few hours from time to time away from the telephone and in privacy just to think. As I do a fair amount of travelling, I find enormous benefit in having time on my own in a hotel room with a foolscap pad just to plan, think, solve and be creative. So, no longer regard thinking time as a luxury, but plan it in as an essential.

Learning time

How about learning time? Reading, preparing new thoughts, digesting information and developing new skills – these are all crucial for success and achievement. If your learning time in a month is currently zero, three or four hours must be allocated. Turn your vehicle into a classroom. I do not travel anywhere without listening to personal development or business CDs. It is incredibly effective and a great use of what could otherwise be fruitless, wasted hours of one's life. Do invest in business and personal development books. They really are a worthwhile investment and the few hours spent studying will reap untold rewards.

Exercise time

How about physical exercise? Are you allocating some time every day to keep the body fit, which in turn helps the brain to perform? It's your life, it's your time – how long do you want to live and what quality of life do you want? When the body ceases to perform, due to neglect or abuse, the quality of life is dramatically lessened. What is the purpose of working incredibly long hours? In many cases, consuming foods, alcohol and tobacco that can be detrimental to your health. And on top of that, the body ceases to function effectively, the quality of life decreases and all that effort and striving is to no avail. There seems very little point in striving for success just to put your body into a wheelchair, a hospital or a grave.

If we imagine our body is like a car battery, without recharging it will go flat – but while one is driving, it is continually being charged. Our bodies as well as our minds need the recharge, so recharging time must be valued and planned. This can be your play time as well as family time. We make better decisions, respond better and become more proactive after recharging time. So, sports, hobbies and interests are an equally essential ingredient in our pursuit of success and therefore happiness.

Our second most valuable asset is our body. For those of us who are fortunate enough to have a healthy and/or complete body, it is our duty and responsibility to take care of it.

PROTECTING YOUR BANK ACCOUNT OF TIME

Try not to waste your time; utilize every waking minute of the day. In addition, do not let other people waste your valuable time. Virtually every successful person, I am sure, would agree that they cannot abide time wasters. Make sure that the finite amount of time we have available, 'our bank account', is not pilfered by others, or indeed by yourself.

Pocket Reminders

- Balance work and play time
- Manage your stress
- Have days of achievement, not activity
- Create a 'to do' list at the end of each day
- Prioritize the list
- Handle interruptions effectively
- Ensure you are able to 'switch off'
- Build 'thinking time' into your schedule
- Build 'learning time' into your schedule
- Build 'exercise time' into your schedule
- Don't procrastinate – do it now!
- Utilize your time and do not allow yourself or others to waste it.

WISE WORDS

Look at a day when you are supremely satisfied at the end. It's not a day when you lounge around doing nothing; it's when you've had everything to do, and you've done it.

Margaret Thatcher

6

Self-management

In order to succeed, any major project needs a process of management. So it is with your project to be successful. The project needs to be managed properly and the only person who can do that is you.

This chapter is about self-management. Self-management is a positive activity and you should be able to embrace the idea more enthusiastically than self-control or self-discipline.

MANAGING YOURSELF

Everybody is a manager. Some people have the responsibility of managing others as well as themselves, but I earnestly believe that in order to be an effective leader or manager of others, one has to master self-management first.

I cannot think of any person who has achieved great success in any given field, be it in business, sport, entertainment or politics, who has not exhibited self-control, self-discipline and self-management. Sadly, prisons throughout the world contain many people who were unable to resist the negative temptations of the world and lacked self-control. Self-control is perhaps best described as thought control, and it is from this stance that we should approach the amazing opportunities that self-management can create for us as we progress towards success and happiness.

Imagine that you have with you at all times – like some head of state – two advisers. Like political advisers they are face-less and invisible, yet you can hear their advice on every-thing you plan to do. We will call these advisers Mr Success and Mr Failure. They work 24 hours a day, and the harder they work, the more persistent they become with their suggestions. These two can totally influence the results and achievement in your life. Ask yourself, who have you been taking advice from for most of your life so far?

Imagine a cold winter's morning. The alarm clock goes off. Mr Success always calls this your 'opportunity clock' because it heralds another day of opportunities to be successful. Mr Failure still calls it an 'alarm clock' as he fears the coming of a new day. Mr Success motivates you by saying, 'Great – another day, let's get cracking', while Mr Failure says, 'Bury the clock, stay in bed for another three-quarters of an hour, it's nice and cosy and warm and you don't really want to get going so early.'

Now, if Mr Failure has been running your life and thoughts for years, you stay in bed, and more than likely Mr Success's enthusiasm for achievement does not even enter your mind.

As a child I was fortunate in having a truly great mother who was incredibly wise; I recall her telling me when I was about six years old that it was the devil on my shoulder that made me leave the towels on the floor instead of hanging them up after a bath. It was the devil who made me throw my clothes on the floor instead of folding them up and putting them on the chair. And she used to say that whenever one was tempted to do things one knew were lazy, uncaring or wasteful, it was the devil creating the temptation. That devil from my childhood can be compared to Mr Failure, trying to push me in the wrong direction and preventing me from achieving goals.

One Saturday afternoon, I was in Stratford-upon-Avon and saw a young man throw the packaging from his Kentucky Fried Chicken meal onto the street, even though there were litter bins not too far away. Who was at work in that young person's mind? Mr Success or Mr Failure? A little bit of self-control and he would have listened to Mr Success and walked the 10 or 20 paces to the litter bin. However, Mr Failure said, 'Finished with it, throw it on the ground; it's the easy option, why bother?' More than likely, in that young person's mind, Mr Failure had been at work for years and Mr Success had never had a look in.

SELF-MANAGEMENT TECHNIQUES

So how can we get Mr Success to work for us? Because as hard as we try, we cannot fire Mr Failure. I have tried and he is always there at some stage or other to find a weakness. All we can do is to try to keep him on sick leave.

The way to develop Mr Success's muscle power and endless determination and enthusiasm will be by providing him with a burning goal (refer also to Chapter 7 – Goals: The Purpose of Life). Self-management, self-discipline and self-control become automatic when we have goals. If the goal is realistic, if it is valid, if we want it far more than anything else, our thought processes and behavioural patterns really do become automatic.

Changing bad habits and routines

Now let us develop these ideas into real practicality. So much of Mr Failure's strength is due to bad habits. In order to change our habits or performance, we must change the patterns or routines behind them. In order to change the result, we must change our patterns and routines. Consider the simplest and easiest way for a smoker to give up smoking. The stages are incredibly simple:

■ Stage one – really decide to stop. You cannot stop if you do not want to.

■ Stage two – break the pattern, change the routine. Although the body requires nicotine, much smoking follows a pattern: after a cup of coffee, in a pub with a beer, before an important telephone call. So, make it easy: choose a time when your routines or patterns are changing anyway – for example, during a two-week holiday. As you get to the airport, that is the last cigarette you will have. Because you have changed the routine and pattern and you are in a new environment, with new activities in new situations, the craving will be dramatically reduced.

During the first two or three days, you may crave a cigarette from time to time. That actual craving only lasts for 10–20 seconds and you will get a message from Mr Failure: 'I want a cigarette.' Just say to yourself, I am a non-smoker, I do not want one, and the craving speedily disappears. Obviously, it will be harder if you are mixing with people who are continually lighting up around you.

The real test is when you return from holiday to the old routine. After two weeks without cigarettes, the craving will have dramatically diminished, with the temptation lasting only a few seconds at a time, so you will have broken out of your original pattern and routine.

A great definition of stupidity is to do the same thing next year as you have done this year and expect a different result.

Admit your weakness

Every one of us has strengths and weaknesses. I am convinced that there is real strength in admitting to and being honest about one's weaknesses. I understand from people who work with alcoholics that treatment can start only when a person is able to admit he or she is an alcoholic. It takes strength and courage to seek help, but the goal of being non-dependent upon alcohol is far more important than Mr Failure urging you to 'have one more drink, it won't do any harm, and why shouldn't you anyhow?'

TEN STEPS TO MASTER SELF-MANAGEMENT

Changing bad habits/routines and admitting your weaknesses are the foundation blocks of self-management, so let us run through 10 stages to effectively reinforce these principles.

1. Control what you say and how you say it

Control what you say – manage the words that come out of your mouth. It is a well-known fact that it is more profitable for us all as individuals to listen than speak (after all, we have two ears and one mouth). Also remember that it is rude to talk at or over the top of other people's conversation. So, you must be able to decide when it is right to keep quiet and listen and when to assert your point of view. Maintaining a balance is the key to fluent conversation, but if this is too hard, keep quiet.

It is a characteristic of the most successful and popular people that they appear to be naturally good listeners. It is self-management – they have achieved a balance between talking and listening.

2. Do not lose self-control

The loss of self-control immediately gives an advantage to other people. Many people waste an enormous amount of power and energy by retaliating through anger, or trying to get their own back.

Ensure your facial expression always has an element of a smile or concentration. If you never show anger, temper or loss of control, you will always maintain credibility, as well as controlling the situation. Lose your temper and you've lost.

So, use your brain and remember, it does not matter what anybody else says, thinks or does – it is what you do that matters.

3. Do the nasty job first

Another tip that I have found useful over the years is to always do the nasty job first. It requires self-discipline, but it is so easy. Mr Failure says, 'Do it later on, get around to doing it, do something more enjoyable.' Mr Success: 'Do it now, get it done and you'll be so pleased once it's been tackled.' Like all good habits, it takes a little while to acquire, but it will soon become automatic.

This is probably the major characteristic of the high achiever – the willingness to tackle the nasty job first. If there is only one piece of advice that you take from this book, take this one – it will reap you untold rewards from less stress to greater respect, from low achievement to high achievement, from weak self-management to self-control, from being unlucky to being lucky.

4. Reward yourself

Having done something nasty or unpleasant, give yourself something to look forward to. Many of us, as children, were promised a sweet by our parents after a dose of disgusting medicine. Do the same thing for yourself: it gives you an incentive to finish the nasty job and move on (after your reward, of course). My reward after an exercise routine is a swim.

5. Use a time-management system

In Chapter 5 – Time: Your Greatest Resource, I demon-strated a very simple time-management system. Mr Failure will encourage you to ignore this. Ask yourself right now: in all honesty, are you using your time as effectively as it could be used? If the answer is negative, Mr Failure is influencing your self-management.

6. Keep yourself in good shape

It makes sense to have a thorough, regular professional health check. But in between these checks we need to keep our bodies in the best shape possible. As I have continually stressed, the brain works better when the body is healthy.

Over the years, I have experienced a few bouts of depres-sion, but when I have been taking regular exercise and my body has been in a strong, extremely healthy and fit state, I have never experienced depression. Although I am not medically qualified to give an opinion on this, I can only give you my experiences and results. So, to enjoy life more, self-manage your body.

7. Avoid over-indulgence

I love eating, I enjoy a drink, I can honestly say that I enjoy most of the temptations that are available, but over-indulgence, in whatever form, is caused by Mr Failure at work, and the results are just what he hopes to achieve, ie lethargy and possibly ill health. Make sure you maintain a balance.

8. Handle procrastination and temptation

Procrastination is putting off getting round to something that one should be doing. I have already suggested that no successful person in any sphere exhibits a high level of procrastination. Procrastination and achievement find it impossible to work together.

Those three little words DO IT NOW are a great self-motivator. Remember the saying 'Don't put off until tomorrow what you can do today.' Put it into action yourself.

9. Say to yourself, 'I have tremendous willpower'

Stop saying, 'I have no willpower, or 'I have very little willpower'. Say instead, 'I have tremendous willpower' – and keep saying it! As you read through this book you will realize the immense importance of this message. Regular, positive affirmation becomes visualized and will eventually create the desired result (and vice versa, of course).

Say to your partner or your children, 'You have tremendous willpower.' That alone will help them to avoid temptation. The willpower that we all wish we had a little more of is available to all of us through self-management. Just try it for 30 days – whenever Mr Failure raises temptation, say, 'I have tremendous willpower', and you will be thrilled with the results.

10. Believe in yourself

Manage your thoughts, your emotions, your joys, your anger and your temper, because every one of us is capable of total self-control. Imagine this little scenario. A husband and wife are furiously arguing when the doorbell rings and there are two friends on the doorstep. How do the couple handle the situation? The one who answers the door immediately controls their temper, facial expression, thoughts and behaviour. As the guests are invited in, the other partner will almost certainly immediately change too. Although there might be a bit of an atmosphere, the actual anger will have been instantly controlled due to the interruption. You see, we can all control ourselves – it just depends how badly we want to.

One of the greatest athletes in the latter half of the 20th century was the British runner Sebastian Coe. I recall hearing him talk about the enormous willpower, self-discipline, self-control and self-management that made him into a world record-holder and Olympic champion in the 800-metre and 1,500-metre races. Even on Christmas morning he had to get out of bed very early to go for his training session. His Christmas dinner was eaten on the understanding that he had another training session shortly afterwards. Every single day he trained relentlessly.

How did Sebastian Coe acquire and develop those attributes? Did he have more willpower than you or I? Was he more self-disciplined? Was his control and self-management more effective than ours? Yes, of course, and may I suggest that this was because of his goal, his vision, and wanting more than anything else to become the Olympic and world champion. Yes, he had paid a price, but he certainly enjoyed the benefits!

In the next chapter, you can discover how to identify your own goals, in order to capitalize on your self-management techniques.

Pocket Reminders

- Listen to Mr Success and put Mr Failure on sick leave
- Be aware that you may have to make sacrifices in order to succeed
- Do not be afraid to change bad habits and routines
- Do not be afraid to admit your weaknesses.

Ten steps to master self-management:

1. Control what you say and how you say it
2. Do not lose self-control in anger or in temper
3. Do the nasty job first
4. Reward yourself
5. Use a time-management system
6. Keep yourself in good shape
7. Avoid over-indulgence
8. Say to yourself, 'I have tremendous willpower'
9. Handle procrastination
10. Believe in yourself.

WISE WORDS

A professional is someone who can do his best work when he does not feel like it.

Alistair Cooke

7

Goals: The Purpose of Life

You can have *anything* you want, but you cannot have *everything*.

You have only 24 hours in a day, you can only ever be in one place at one time and you have only so many years on this planet. So you literally cannot have it all, even if you were foolish enough to consider it feasible.

If you desire success, you need to have clear ambitions. The whole principle of achieving success is to translate your desires into the results that you want. This is called setting goals.

WHAT IS A GOAL?

The *Oxford English Dictionary* defines a goal as 'the object of a person's ambition or effort... a destination... an aim'. This is, of course, exactly the simplicity of this message.

Everyone must have an aim, a destination that one is trying to arrive at. Let me quote again that simple but truthful cliché: 'A person going nowhere gets there.'

Goals of survival and goals of achievement

Everybody has some sort of goal. Of course, there are extremes. Some people do not think beyond their next meal. For others, their goal is a drink of alcohol, and for many their goal is just to get through the day – these are goals of survival. At the other extreme are the great human achievements: the one-tenth of a second shaved off a world record, the acquisition of a multi-million-pound company, the perfection of a piece of music or work of art. Between these two extremes we find the majority of us who, unfortunately, have a poor ratio of goals of achievement as against goals of survival.

The purpose of your life is not to let the circumstances of life push and pull you. It is for *you to decide* what *you* want your life to be. This chapter will enable you to set horizons towards which you will progress. Your journey to success is towards the goals that you will set for yourself, and the fuel that will power you towards your goals is the strength of the desire that you have to achieve your success. This chapter is thus of vital importance to you in becoming as successful as you wish.

Realistic goals

Let me stress again, you can have anything you *really* want *if* you set it as your goal.

Note that I have emphasized the word 'really'. We all go through life seeing and hearing of things we would like to do. We often think, 'If only I could do that', or 'If only I could have that', but ask yourself the question – is that what you *really* want? I could not be a ballet dancer, nor would I want to be: I am a wee bit too old, my body is the wrong shape and anyhow, it does not motivate or inspire me, and even if it did, we have to get our ambitions into perspective – we have to be positive realists.

Although goals must be ambitious, they must also be achievable. Distinguish between the goals of achievement and the goals of survival, ie everyday activities.

We invariably acquire the things we really want and we achieve the ambitions we really aspire to. The majority of your personal acquisitions have been gained because you really wanted them. The success or achievement in your life to date will have come about almost certainly because you really wanted that achievement. If that is so, then goals for the future can easily be set and the achievement of those goals will become automatic by using the techniques set out in this chapter.

Achievement through goals

Without goals, nothing can be achieved. There is not one single success story that was not goal inspired. Whether we look at sporting achievements, mountain climbing, medical research, computer technology, warfare, music, the arts or business, every achievement is goal inspired. In some cases, owing to urgency and even fear, humankind's creativity and inspiration achieves advancement that hitherto may have been beyond realistic capability.

The benefits to humankind are limitless. A classic example is Formula 1 motor racing. Improvements in the performance and safety of the family car are a direct result of the relentless drive to improve the racing car and win the next Grand Prix. The materials developed to send humans to outer space and back safely have not only enhanced our domestic air travel beyond imagining, but some of those materials have become part of everyday life in the kitchen. Humankind's relentless drive for more sophisticated and deadly weapons has also had a positive result with the use of lasers in our hospitals.

Although weaponry seems a rather negative example, it is in no way meant to glorify warfare – it merely illustrates the point that necessity truly is the mother of invention, and if we can do it in that field, we can surely advance and achieve new pinnacles of 'success' for more positive outcomes.

POSITIVE GOALS

Earlier I talked about happiness. One of the main criteria for happiness is having something to look forward to, ie hope.

Retirement

Many people look forward to retiring at some stage in their life. In my work, I continually find people whose sole purpose seems to be retirement. The last three or four years of their careers are used up in progressing towards this utopia. I hear of the frustrations of many senior managers and chief executives in motivating these types of people. What is tragic is that they are no good to themselves and are a barrier to other people's success.

Many people in this category are unwilling to change, convince themselves they cannot take on new ideas, and lose all their capacity to inspire, motivate and lead others. In many cases, what happens in reality is that after retirement individuals find themselves in a vacuum with nothing to look forward to. The tragedy is that many of them die within one year, or suffer through ill health, inactivity, boredom and mental stagnation – their purpose has gone.

None of us should ever retire – all that we should do, at some stage of our lives, is stop working for a living. Retirement is only the beginning of a new life, which must be planned and driven by goals to provide the 'always have something to look forward to'.

There are numerous examples of people in their retirement years achieving almost unbelievable results. There was Babs Hiscock, who didn't take up running until she was 63 and by the age of 84 had completed some 26 marathons. Colonel Sanders didn't start his Kentucky Fried Chicken business until he had retired, bored and frustrated, at the age of 63, and there are numerous examples of authors who didn't write their first books until after retirement. Finally, the Queen Mother was still keeping up her public appearances, travelling by helicopter, making speeches and bringing untold joy to countless thousands of people in the second century of her life.

Setting positive goals

So, why do such things that we are all so familiar with happen? Very simply, people fail to set positive goals, develop interests, hobbies or new activities that they can look forward to.

The reason that you have progressed so far in this book must be that you have it within you to set goals and achieve success. Success and achievement must really appeal to you; and yet there are countless people who cynically dismiss the goal of success, because they have been conditioned throughout their lives to believe it is only for others, not for them.

DETERMINING SUCCESS – THE IMPORTANCE OF DESIRE

A number of years ago I attended a training session in the Regency Hyatt Hotel in Chicago with some 2,000 other people. A great speaker, Peter Riggs, made this powerful statement: 'It's desire, not ability, that determines your success. You can get anything, you can do anything if you really want to; the only limitation is what you put on yourself.'

This statement has helped and motivated me ever since. Desire is the fuel that drives you forward towards the destination which is represented by your goals.

EDUCATION AND KNOWLEDGE

I was brought up conditioned to believe that success was all about academic ability. Even though a brilliant education was made available to me, it did not appeal. I spent far too much time playing sport and being involved with the Cadet Force. I found schoolwork to be an annoying interruption to the other activities. I did not gain any A levels or a university education. I left school with just enough O levels (GCSEs today) to get into an agricultural college, as my ambition was to be a farmer and I believed that my expectations of life must have a ceiling.

We have many examples of young people leaving school, having failed their exams, with no career in mind. They may spend time on various government schemes before finding a job or a career that they really want to take up. They often go to evening classes or to a place of further education and retake the exams that they had previously failed, and this time pass with an excellent result. Why? Has their ability changed? No, of course not – their desire has changed.

How important is education?

According to a survey of the top 20 most successful entrepreneurs, only 4 went to university. Two more had experienced some formal business training. The remainder went through the 'university of life', but the survey went on to report that even though some 70 per cent were not highly educated, they all regretted it.

These statistics show that university education is not a prerequisite for amassing money. I am in no way deriding university education. As a parent, it was one of my dearest wishes for all my sons to go to university, but only one gained a BA. Nevertheless, education, without question, in all its various forms, whether formal or otherwise, is not a prerequisite for success and achievement.

I once had great difficulty in accepting the following statement: 'Formal education has one purpose only in life and that is to get us our first job – self-education earns us our living.' Initially, I felt this statement was a total devaluation of everything that an education system sets out to do, but of course it is right. The school, college and university years are immensely important, but the actual knowledge gained during those years is not necessarily of use in providing students with their standard of living. It therefore becomes even more important that the knowledge and experiences gained after leaving formal education become more valuable from a monetary future viewpoint.

Applying knowledge

Once again, I must stress that it is desire that is overwhelmingly important – ability, skill or knowledge can be gained later on. Many people overestimate the power of knowledge. While essential in the academic world, in a business environment it is only potential power – we are paid for what we *do* with our knowledge. Many young people leaving education find this to be a dramatic setback to their beliefs and understanding. For many, their confidence and self-image has been totally dependent upon education and they have worked hard to gain qualifications that are of value in gaining interviews and obtaining jobs, but of little practical use until that knowledge can be applied practically.

THE IMPORTANCE OF SETTING GOALS

So, why is it that so few people set goals, and why is goal setting not taught at school, college and university? Why are our great seats of learning not teaching their students that they can have anything they want? This of course is an immensely complex question, and one that is beyond the remit of this book, but suffice it to say that educationalists almost certainly have not been taught the value of goal setting themselves.

Generally, people do not set goals because they do not believe they can get what they want. They believe that other people can achieve their goals, but not them. This in turn produces a poor self-image, as I described earlier.

If by now you accept the premise that it is desire, not ability, that determines our success, how do you build up your desire? You build desire by setting goals.

It is vital to have goals – one could almost say that we could not live without them. One must also understand that it is not the actual goal that is important as long as we have one – even if it turns out to be the wrong goal. Buckminster Fuller, a brilliant, creative person, talked about the law of precision, and he described this as the principle that in addition to gaining a goal, one gains many experiences, personal growth, confidence and knowledge in the process.

For example, a young person attending university might spend three to six years gaining their degree. The degree, of course, is the goal, but in the process of acquiring it, that person will have built many relationships that will last their lifetime. The knowledge and experience gained by studying for the degree may also prove invaluable in later years. So, actually having a goal almost creates a personal development system in its own right.

While striving towards any goal you will almost certainly encounter setbacks. There will be unforeseen circumstances and there will, of course, be days when you are tempted to say, 'Just my luck', but a person striving towards that goal transcends those setbacks and in the process builds the principles of philosophy and achievement. The setbacks in themselves are a major part of personal growth and development. We will be looking at this further in Chapter 11 – Overcoming Setbacks.

How to devise goals

Let us now progress to the goal-setting programme so you can decide what it is you *really* want, and how to build the desire, ie the energy and the fuel for achievement.

1. Goals must be ambitious but achievable

Goals must be ambitious, but also within our reach. Everyday activities are not goals. A goal is something that you really want, but are currently not experiencing. If you do not change anything in your life you will not experience anything different.

2. Make a list of all your goals

Make a list of the things that you really want. This list should be divided into long-term and mid-term as well as short-term goals. The list can contain what some may classify as really big goals, and should include goals in your business life and your private life. Don't forget goals for personal development: hobbies, sports and social activities. These goals can be tangible, such as acquiring possessions and money, as well as intangible, like health and fitness, or the ability to inspire and communicate. This can be an enjoyable and entertaining exercise, but it is not a game – it is a deadly serious activity that is essential for success.

Most people indulge in the luxury of 'goal thoughts' only when dreaming about winning the lottery or the football pools: 'We'll buy a new house, a new car, go on a cruise.' For many, that is the sum of their exposure to goal setting.

I have said you can have anything you **really want** – but do you know what it is that you really want? By following this second stage you can list the goals that you want to achieve.

3. Discuss your goals with your partner

If you share your life with somebody else, this exercise must be done together. Two people with goals, some of which may be different and some of which they hold in common, become an incredibly powerful winning force. But if they have a completely separate list of goals that are not shared, this may become a recipe for conflict in the future.

Partners do not have to have the same interests, hobbies, goals or ambitions, but there must be some fundamental goals that they share. This then gives each partner in that relationship understanding and respect for the other's goals and ambitions, and there is strength in that they are shared together.

4. Ensure you set your own goals

Set goals that *you* really want, not wishes that other people may aspire to, and do not feel pressurized by media hype. They must be *your* goals; it is your life. Be realistic if money is involved (we will discuss monetary goals in the last chapter – Financial Success).

5. Set deadlines

Decide when exactly you want to achieve a certain goal. Goal setting and achievement are not effective without a timescale. The brain is not fuelled or energized, it cannot respond, without a deadline. Start off with the year, move on to the month and then to the precise date.

6. Carry your list of goals with you

Write down and carry with you this list of goals. I have found over the years that compiling a list of goals, especially for the first time, takes time. It may take several hours, even days or weeks. This does not matter, but having put the time in and having experienced the sheer excitement of concentrating on what we want to do rather than what we do not want to do, we must not waste this effort.

Write that complete list down with the date alongside each goal. Some of those goals may be for 10 or 20 years hence. Some of the goals on your very first list will change with time. Many of us, at the end of a year, think about our goals for the forthcoming year. Some of these will change as the year develops, due to circumstances that may be outside our immediate control. Further guidance on this is provided at the end of the chapter.

7. Be flexible when planning your goals

Don't be afraid to adapt your goals as new information, new experiences and new knowledge come along.

8. Give up things that are barriers to your goal

Give up anything that is in direct opposition to your goal. Remember what I said in Chapter 6 – Self-management: if you have to change your patterns and routines and if you feel you are making a sacrifice, remember, it is not a sacrifice, it is a step towards your goal, which is much more important to you than whatever you are going to sacrifice. Do not, under any circumstances, allow past habits, weaknesses or procrastination to block the path to your success, achievement and happiness.

9. Be careful with whom you share your goals

By all means share with anybody what can best be described as 'give up' goals, such as losing weight, becoming fitter, or anything else that relates to personal development. But regarding goals that relate to personal advancement and acquisitions, be very careful whom you tell. There are many people who will be supportive of your attempts to become fitter or to lose weight, but who will be extremely negative towards your making more money, having a better lifestyle, driving a new car.

Unfortunately, jealousy is one of the worst human characteristics. It eats away at people by generating continual negative thoughts and energy, which could otherwise be used towards achieving success and happiness.

10. Start to visualize your goals

Picture yourself actually having attained your goals. In Chapter 9 – Using Visualization, we will discuss this in more detail, but please do not dismiss this stage. When I first learnt about goals, I had great difficulty imagining I had achieved them when I knew perfectly well that I had not. Keep in mind that wonderful quotation 'Whatever the mind of man can accurately conceive and believe, it is forced to achieve.'

If one of your goals is promotion, which involves greater responsibility, imagine yourself in that position. How would you dress? Visualize yourself in that particular office; see yourself speaking and making the decisions.

WRITING OUT YOUR GOALS

Take some time to write down your goals. You can use the box on the next page to make a list.

Discuss your goals with your partner if you have one and distinguish between the ones you have in common and those that are personal to you.

Separate your business goals from your personal goals, asking yourself, 'What do I really want?', and then be realistic, but not unambitious.

Remember to put realistic dates against each goal, whether tangible or intangible.

MY GOALS		
Work	**Personal**	**Target date**

Long-term:

Mid-term:

Short-term:

Pocket Reminders

- You can have anything that you really want
- Decide what you want your life to be
- Remember, a person going nowhere normally gets there
- It is desire rather than knowledge and ability that determines your success.

Ten tips on setting goals:

1. Your goals must be ambitious but achievable
2. Make a list of all your goals
3. Discuss your goals with your partner
4. Ensure that you set *your own* goals
5. Set deadlines
6. Carry with you your list of goals
7. Be flexible when planning your goals
8. Give up things that are barriers to your goals
9. Be careful with whom you share your goals
10. Start to visualize your goals.

WISE WORDS

Every person is a self-made person, but only the successful ones admit it.

8

Personal Planning

I am sure you have heard the much-used cliché 'People don't plan to fail, they fail to plan.'

Imagine the holiday of a lifetime that so many of us wish for. That holiday could well include a journey by cruise ship. Imagine meeting the captain of that ship and asking him which route the ship would be taking to its destination and his replying, 'I'm not sure, we haven't thought about that yet, I really don't know, but don't worry, I'm sure somebody else does.'

What if the captain had no detailed plan of routes and of ports of call, or was not aware of the resources available? That ship would be destroyed on some rocky coastline. Would you travel with this captain if you knew he had no plan? Of course not. So, why should your life be any different?

The above analogy emphasizes, I hope, the importance of personal planning.

The plans and goals that you set become the purpose of your life. The stronger and more enthusiastic your desire for the goal, the more likely you are to achieve it. There is nothing wrong with that. I suggested earlier that power comes from organized energy and effort. Achieving the plan is utilizing that power within you.

PEOPLE WITH PURPOSE

It is easy to spot people with purpose. You can tell them by the way they walk, the way they hold their heads and their overall body language.

Have you ever looked down onto a busy street? I once looked out of a window down onto a busy street in central London. The pavements were full of people all seeming to be rushing from one store to another. It seemed as though everybody had a purpose, but what was so amazing was how few collisions there were. By contrast, have you ever noticed, while on holiday, other holidaymakers doing what one could call the 'holiday walk'? It is something that most people naturally seem to slip into. I bet you have been frustrated with the 'holiday driver' ambling along, admiring the hedgerow and driving all the other motorists who have a job to do, a time schedule to keep and a goal to achieve, completely and utterly potty! These people cause frustration, which can lead to accidents, because they have no purpose or plan.

PRIORITIZING

In Chapter 7 – Goals, I discussed the most effective system for planning and prioritizing the key objectives of each day. With this sort of self-discipline and planning, your life and goals become very systematic. I will state it once again: every success is the result of a plan.

Your 'corporate' plan

The Japanese business community was held to be an example of success and efficiency from the 1950s through to the 1990s. Most analysts and business teachers agree that one of the most important factors in Japanese industry's vast growth and success has been its use of longer-term plans, over 15 and 20 years, and investment which was not expected to provide returns in the short term.

In the United Kingdom, the business community has been plagued by shareholders' demands for immediate return: they want high dividends and spare no thought for the long-term growth and investment that is needed for better success.

Well, you might say, what has all this got to do with me and my success? '..........................' Limited (write your name in here). Would you be a good investment for outsiders? Are you going to have a plan and a strategy? Will you give a fair return for the investment in the long run? This, of course, does not just relate to money, it relates to what you can put back into the community.

I am convinced there are more opportunities around now than there have ever been. Why? Because the world has become smaller – obviously not literally, but due to improved communication. Air travel, telephone and radio communications have all played their part. In Europe, certainly, people are well aware of what is going on in the rest of the world. As more and more nations open their borders, increased trade has created vast new opportunities.

As people have more money to spend, opportunities are created. People are living longer and this creates more opportunity. People's concerns over their health and fitness create more opportunity. People having more time for leisure, and hence the incredible growth of sports and hobbies, creates new opportunity. People's thirst for knowledge creates new opportunity. This is all available to you if you just care to look.

Creating the master plan

So, how does one go about creating the master plan and then the detailed support plan for each goal? Well, like everything else it is incredibly simple and just downright common sense. These are the main principles:

1. Set a deadline

I stressed the importance of setting a date or deadline for each goal. Ideally, the maximum time is three months. Yes, of course you can have long-term objectives, but in order to motivate yourself, the shorter the time period, the better. A very large goal should be broken down into more easily managed, short timescales.

Imagine you are going to catch a plane next Thursday at 7 pm and today is Saturday. You may feel excited, but as far as adrenalin flow, extra effort and personal self-motivation go, the departure time is of little significance at this stage. On Thursday, the time of departure takes on a greater significance. By midday, every effort is being made to remove any barriers that might stop you getting you to the airport on time. By around about 5 pm it is all systems go. It is amazing how very few people ever miss a plane!

You must manage your most valuable asset, your brain. Set it too big a goal in too short a timeframe and the resulting non-achievement becomes a powerful negative influence, leading to disillusionment.

The importance of this message is twofold. First, aim to have a cut-off time, and secondly, remember that the greater proportion of effort is put in as the cut-off time gets closer. We are motivated when the goal is not too far away.

2. Break the plan down into easily achievable stages

Another phrase that has had a direct impact on my life is the cliché 'Success by the inch is a cinch, and by the yard it is hard.' I learnt this many years ago as being one of the laws of success and still teach the importance of that message to this day.

If someone asked you, 'Could you walk from London to Brighton?', your reply would almost certainly be 'I don't think I could do that.' So let me ask this another way: 'Could you walk five miles in one day?' Your reply almost certainly would be 'Yes, I could do that.' So in 10 days you could have completed the journey.

This illustrates why it is so important to break very big goals down into realistic, achievable stages.

3. Be prepared to change direction

You must be prepared to change the route or direction of your goal, if necessary. You do not have to *change* the goal, but the way it is achieved or planned may need on occasion to be changed owing to external influences which may be outside your control. But you must take care as this is a great opportunity for Mr Failure to find an excuse.

What I mean by external influences over which you have no control are such things as government policy, interest rate changes, redundancy, the public not buying your products as fashion changes. Such uncontrollable factors may make it necessary to change the direction of your plans.

History is full of people and organizations that through stubbornness, short-sightedness or stupidity are unwilling to change direction in order to achieve their goals. I recall a conversation with a major international publisher and my question was 'What business are you in?' and the reply was 'Publishing books.' My next question was 'What is your goal?' 'To publish books that people will read', he replied. 'Yes, I'm sure you're right', I said. 'But surely your business is not just the publishing of books but the selling of books, because without sales you'll have no business?'

If a company's long-term plan is to stay in business and make profits for reinvestment and security, as well as for shareholders and investors, it may have to look for new markets and new sales opportunities. Similarly, we must consider our long-term goals and be prepared to change direction if necessary.

4. Check your plan regularly to ensure you are on the right course

Most plans should be broken down into various stages, with scheduled completion dates. Are you on course or is a bit more effort required? Have you missed a deadline or are you ahead of schedule? Do check regularly where you are on your plan and, indeed, if you are still on the right course.

5. Concentrate your thoughts

Remember to concentrate your thoughts on what you want, rather than what you do not want. If you catch yourself thinking about the latter, instantaneously change that thought and replace it with what you *do* want.

6. Build support for your plans

If you are not receiving support from your partner, try to understand their viewpoint. This may require discussion in order to stamp out any selfish behaviour on your part. I am not saying that you should forsake your plans, but a little bit of effort to build the support and create team spirit will be well worthwhile.

7. Only ask the opinions of those who are qualified

It is perfectly normal to seek opinions or advice when attempting to solve a problem or prepare a plan of action, but be careful who you ask. I was faced with a fantastic money-making opportunity when I was 32, and having stayed awake all night weighing up the pros and cons (as this opportunity required some considerable investment which I would have to borrow), naturally I sought opinions. I discussed it with my solicitor, accountant and bank manager and they all strongly advised me against it. With the greatest respect, it occurred to me that perhaps their opinions in this instance were of little value, as none of them had any money or had any experience of the business I was going to invest in.

So, I borrowed the money and got cracking – I might add that it proved to be a very successful exercise. If you are looking for advice or opinions, always ask yourself, 'Is this opinion really worth listening to?' Consider the experience or qualifications of the person you are asking.

8. Consider what you have to do to achieve your goal

Now create the plan. This is the most enjoyable part of the exercise. It can be a personal brainstorming session. In Chapter 2 – Your Greatest Asset, I suggested that you ask yourself for ideas and solutions. In preparing your plan, ask yourself the key question:

'What do *I* have *to do* to achieve .... (your goal)'.

The ideas then unfold. Just put them on a sheet of paper so you can prioritize them when you finalize your plan.

9. Ensure your plan is visible at all times

Ensure your goal plan is visible – at least to you. The ship's captain has a chartroom and chart table with a route plan clearly visible at all times; any pilot will be able to tell you, at any given time, exactly where they are on that plan, to within a few feet.

An example of a plan

I wanted to create an example of a goal plan and to make it as simple as possible. I have selected as an example the goal of losing weight. For those of you who have no interest in losing weight, just apply the same principles to any goal, eg getting a job, getting promoted, acquiring personal fitness, a new car or holiday cottage, a company takeover, running your own business, being a top performer, or any achievement in any sphere. It is the principle that is important.

Current weight: 15 stone Goal weight: 13 stone 10 lb Date 1 August	Tick when completed
1. Buy pair of training shoes £40.00	20 May
2. Buy tracksuit £30.00	27 May
3. Have medical check with GP	29 May
4. Plan diet & exercise routine	31 May
5. Start on diet	1 June
6. Start on exercise routine (20 min per day)	1 June
7. Current weight: 14 stone 12 lb	6 June
8. Current weight: 14 stone 10 lb	13 June
9. Current weight: 14 stone 8 lb	20 June
10. Increase exercise (30 min per day)	
11. Change diet	

12.	Current weight: 14 stone 6 lb	27 June
13.	Current weight: 14 stone 4 lb	3 July
14.	Current weight: 14 stone 2 lb	10 July
15.	Current weight: 14 stone 0 lb	17 July
16.	Current weight: 13 stone 12 lb	24 July
17.	Current weight: 13 stone 10 lb	30 July

Pocket Reminders

- Set a deadline

- Break the plan down into easily achievable stages

- Be prepared to change direction

- Check the plan regularly to ensure you are on the right course

- Concentrate your thoughts on what you want

- Build support for your plans

- Ask opinions only from those who are qualified

- Consider what you have to do to achieve your goal

- Ensure your plan is visible at all times.

WISE WORDS

The person who is sure nothing can be done is usually the person who has never done anything.

Bits and Pieces

9

Using Visualization

It has to be said that the satisfaction and excitement you gain from having goals and plans is that as you achieve your goals your confidence grows alongside your competence and skills and this encourages you to set even bigger goals. You know the expression 'Seeing ourselves progressing motivates us.'

When I first learnt about goal setting some years ago, I was told the importance of imagining I had achieved the goal. Initially, I had great difficulty with this. I thought, 'How can I imagine I have achieved it when I haven't?' Being a realist, I found this a major hurdle to overcome. Then I had an experience that totally convinced me of the truth and the power of vivid imagination.

My wife and I decided to sell our farm and move to a house in Bedfordshire that we had fallen in love with. As with all such transactions, there were a number of hurdles to overcome: selling our existing property, raising the necessary mortgage (as it was more than we could afford at the time), trying to avoid being gazumped. This purchase was a rather ambitious goal, but I can tell you that the picture of that house was vividly burnt into my mind: I imagined driving up to it, where the car would go, I could see the routes I would be taking to the office, I could picture every single detail of where our furniture would go. I pictured sleeping, eating, and enjoying every aspect that this prospect offered.

Well, we did have major difficulties in the purchase. I had to work extremely hard to raise the necessary funds and we were under enormous pressure to get the contracts exchanged on time, but we did complete the purchase.

VISUALIZATION TECHNIQUES

From that personal experience, I now totally understand and believe in the importance of visualizing what it is you really want, because today we talk less about goal imagination than goal visualization.

Practical methods

I want to stick to ideas, systems and thoughts that I have tested and found worked for me and for countless thousands of others. Fundamentally, these principles really do not change. People may give them new names, but peel away the verbiage and the principle is the same underneath.

Henry Ford, who is always held to be one of the great success stories, is quoted as saying, 'If you think you can, or you think you can't – you're right.' That is fundamentally correct. Let me repeat, once again, the only limitations are the ones you impose on yourself.

Negative visualization

How often have you heard people say:

- 'I knew I wouldn't win.'
- 'I knew I couldn't do that.'
- 'I knew that ball would go into the bunker.'
- 'I knew I wouldn't get that job.'
- 'I knew I wouldn't get that sale.'
- 'This is going to be a bad month/week/day.'
- 'I don't see myself winning that race.'

These are just a few examples of negative visualization. Any person with these types of thought is absolutely certain to achieve that negative result. 'I knew I wouldn't' – if that thought is in the forefront of your mind, it is almost pointless to proceed, because that alone will make the goal impossible to achieve.

Positive visualization

The first time in the history of human endeavour that the power of visualization was fully exemplified was in the story of Roger Bannister running a mile in under four minutes in 1954. Up until that time, nobody had ever run a mile in under four minutes. It was generally believed it could not be done. While at Oxford University, Roger Bannister had run a quarter of a mile in under a minute on numerous occasions and he visualized putting together these four quarters and running a mile in under four minutes. Well, we all know the result.

What was so amazing about that achievement was that his body had not changed, and there were no new running tracks or track shoes. His mindset, his belief and his visualization had most certainly changed. I am sure he knew he was going to break the four-minute mile record.

If he can – I can

Interestingly, within days, people were running the mile in under four minutes, because Roger Bannister had given them the chance to believe they could. The 'If he can, I can' attitude was exemplified. He visualized and the followers after that first epic event did not have to use their imagination. Their mindset had gone through a dramatic change.

So, visualization can be positive as well as negative. Unfortunately, it is more commonly used negatively. How often have you found yourself worrying about things you do not want? The more you visualize the failure scenario, the more certain it is that this is the scenario which will come about.

There is that well-known saying 'What you fear may come upon you.' We will look at this in more detail in Chapter 11 – Overcoming Setbacks.

Positive, creative visualization is one of the stages in your success plan and this entails consciously maintaining the image of what you want to achieve.

Throughout our lives, we unconsciously use visualization. Virtually everything we do and achieve, we have thought about beforehand. To achieve your success, you must wilfully and determinedly switch negative visualization into positive visualization.

Active positive visualization

If you catch yourself thinking, worrying or seeing yourself in a situation that you do not want to be in, immediately replace that thought with a situation that you do want to be in.

The brain visualizes pictures rather than words. Of course, we communicate with words, but these are instantaneously transposed into pictorial images in our mind. In Chapter 3 – Believe in Yourself, I discussed self-image: people who succeed have a great self-image and people who fail have a miserable self-image.

If you can vividly see yourself having achieved your goal, it will become a reality.

Steve Redgrave is an awesome example of human endeavour – the greatest Olympian Britain has ever produced, the only athlete to have won gold medals at five consecutive Olympic Games. His vision, as with all winners, was paramount. He alone believed he could.

Muhammad Ali is another of the world's all-time great sportspeople. He lost only two fights in the whole of his professional boxing career and will remain in history as possibly the greatest boxer of all time. He told how having met his opponent, he would spend time in uninterrupted thought to concentrate on the forthcoming fight until he could clearly see in his mind himself winning. He visualized the result. He would then hold a press conference and announce in verse which round he would win in, and he was invariably right. He never once in his career said, 'I am going to be the greatest'; he only ever said, 'I am the greatest'.

In Chapter 7 – Goals, I discussed goal selection, but now you must clearly visualize that goal.

Visualize goals

You must define your goals in great detail. For example, you may want a second family car. Now get the detail right. Is it new or used; what make, model, colour, how much, what extras? Now see yourself driving it, visualize parking it, the journeys you will take in it. Get a complete picture of owning and driving that vehicle. Get an exact picture so that your brain can visualize it in every detail. This principle applies to every single goal.

Affirmations

If using self-image and visualization are so important, how do we continually use this knowledge positively and effectively? The answer has already been disclosed through affirmations. Most affirmations begin with 'I am...', and if from today you are sufficiently strong-willed never to make another negative affirmation to yourself, the results will, I promise you, be amazing.

Here are some examples of when you can change negative affirmations into positive affirmations:

- 'I'm feeling ill' – 'I'm feeling fantastic'.
- 'I am broke' – 'I am financially secure'.
- 'I am unhappy' – 'I am happy'.
- 'I'm a lousy skier' – 'I'm a good skier'.
- 'I'm a bad parent' – 'I'm a good parent'.
- 'I'm not a very good husband/wife' – 'I am a good, caring, loving husband/wife'.
- 'I hate doing the housework' – 'I love doing the housework'.

You could keep adding to the list.

If this is the very first time you have encountered these ideas, you cannot help but be sceptical, as I was initially. The subconscious mind needs to be fed the right information. Imagine a vast oak tree; you can see the trunk, branches and leaves, but holding up that tree is an incredible root system that could travel for 30 or 40 yards. Another analogy would be an iceberg: only a tiny proportion is visible compared to the mass that is below sealevel. It is our subconscious that programs us; it moves our muscles when we walk, turns us over in bed, influences almost every single bodily function. So, every experience is recorded in our subconscious ready for use at a later stage.

Many of us have difficulty remembering names. We may know the name, but have difficulty in the recall. This is compounded when we say, 'I'm just bad at remembering' or 'I can't remember'. So this is why it is so important to consistently and consciously think, talk and visualize your success – so that it is totally implanted into your subconscious. Equally, you will find how miraculous the subconscious can be in solving problems or overcoming difficulties.

I have to admit that when I went through the process initially I mouthed affirmation a couple of times and then set off to seek another success system. But as time has gone by, I have resorted to systematically using positive affirmations, and they work!

You do not even have to say these affirmations aloud. Give your brain positive affirmations as you are going to sleep and it will store these messsages in the subconscious. Positive affirmations should be your first thought in the morning: repeat them several times a day. Let me state once again, you owe it to yourself to gradually tip the balance from the negative to the positive, until such time as the negative becomes a rarity.

Just one cautionary statement: affirmations must be positive statements of the present: 'I am successful', 'I am happy', never 'I want to be happy' or, even worse, 'I am going to be happy'.

Sporting analogies are useful in illustrating messages of personal development. With the amazing rewards available for outstanding performance, coaches and athletes seek, then test, every single idea and process that might help them to win. Hardly a week goes by without some new record being shattered. I accept that people train harder and longer and that in team sports, new skills are developed and match-play tactics are skilfully practised and planned. The will to win is enhanced by the desire for the rich rewards of goal achievement.

This cannot be explained away by the evolution of the human body, but I am sure it can be accepted as reality by the development of the human brain in the way that people think.

Scientific research has shown that when we visualize ourselves carrying out a specific activity our brain programs alter as if we were actively performing. There are electro-chemical changes in the cells which produce new behaviour.

Mental rehearsals

I have found that the more I mentally rehearse in total concentration, closing my eyes and visualizing the perfect result, the better the activity is when performed. One of the fastest ways to improve anything in our lives is to join together physical and mental activity and then to practise consistently.

A very good example of this is in the work of actors and actresses. They not only learn the words, but also mentally rehearse the character. They see themselves in their parts and use their imagination to allow themselves to be what many of us would describe as Jekyll and Hyde personalities. When they are playing the role, they become a completely different person.

Coaches and personal development trainers train athletes how to visualize results. For example, a golfer will concentrate on exactly where he or she is going to place the ball, to visualize that perfect shot. So it is with snooker and tennis players. When a player says, 'I knew that I'd do that', it is as a result of positive visualization and subsequent action.

Pocket Reminders

- Define your goals in detail
- Clearly visualize what you want, not what you do not want
- Let your mind visualize achieving those goals
- Stop making negative affirmations
- Practise positive affirmations
- Mentally rehearse
- Have faith in your subconscious and let it work for you.

WISE WORDS

Change your thoughts and you will change your world.

10

The Success Attitude

All the successful people I have met over the years have one thing in common: a 'success attitude'.

This topic is worth considering because whatever sphere of activity successful people operate in, they all seem to have this common trait.

Richard Branson (Virgin), Charles Dunstone (Carphone Warehouse) and Julian Richer (Richer Sounds) are all self-made multimillionaires of the 21st century. The one thing they and all the other successful entrepreneurs have in common is a success attitude. They didn't acquire this once they had achieved their monetary wealth.

All outstanding athletes, musicians, singers and entertainers also exhibit a success attitude, as do the self-made million-aires and billionaires throughout history, and I do not believe that any of them acquired their success attitude *after* they achieved success.

It really is almost the only thing they have in common. So, what is the vital ingredient of your own success attitude? Of course, it is a positive outlook or attitude.

Positive attitude

It is all very well saying we have to be positive. I am certain every one of us agrees that it is essential, but what is a positive attitude? How can I get it? If I have got it, how can I keep it? Once again I thought it helpful to refer to the *Oxford English Dictionary* in attempting to define what a positive attitude really is: 'Constructive; directional. Marked by the presence, rather than the absence, of qualities. Tending in a direction, naturally or arbitrarily taken as that of increase or progress... (of a person) convinced, confident.'

To sum all this up and put it into a simple and memorable form, the success attitude is expressed by a mind that is purposeful, that is expecting the best, is realistically optimistic and is cheerful.

Joan Denny, in the latter part of her life, suffered enormously with arthritic pain to the extent that she became crippled and used a walking stick and a wheelchair from time to time, but she was always incredibly cheerful.

Her house always seemed to be full of visitors. On the days when she decided to stay in bed a little longer, her grandsons would visit her in her room, and I would see four boys all under the age of 10 all over the bed: she would be reading one a story, playing cards with another, pretending to be a battleship with another and cradling one that had dropped off to sleep, all at the same time.

She never burdened any member of her family with her pain or her troubles and on the really bad days, when

> any of us enquired, her reply would be 'The old legs are playing up a bit today.' Her positive and cheerful attitude was a magnet that attracted everyone to her. She may have had pain, but she was never lonely and was always loved.

So, a success attitude creates success and is most certainly acquired before the success has been achieved. At the beginning of this book, I linked happiness to success. We need to draw a distinction between pleasure and happiness. Pleasure is an experience of enjoyment that one has at any given time, but does not really have any long-lasting effect. We get pleasure from hobbies, music, playing a sport, enjoying a meal, a beautiful sunset or the smell of flowers – the list is endless. These are the pleasures of life which one strives to enjoy – and, combined together, they can create happiness.

Make yourself happy

Linking happiness and success together in developing the success attitude should, of course, be your main goal. Who decides whether you are going to be happy or unhappy?

Are you dependent upon the morning news as to whether you are going to be happy or unhappy that day? Are you dependent upon the government, or the weather, or your partner or what arrives in the post?

Will Rogers said most people are about as happy as they make up their minds to be. You and I know that we can be in control of our minds if we want to be.

Truth and honesty

I have found that people who are honest with themselves are automatically able to be honest with their fellows. In almost every single situation, our happiness is dependent on our relationships with others.

The more effective and better our communication, the greater the trust and respect we receive and the greater the happiness we can achieve.

People who are not honest with others experience stress and have low self-esteem. They are nearly always non-achievers. So much time is wasted covering up a lie or remembering what one said last time. From a parental point of view, I am sure it must be one of the strongest principles that can be embedded in a child's brain: the strength and the security of being truthful and honest with others.

From a communication point of view, the truth may be hard to say at times, but my goodness it is easy to remember, and it is so much nicer to deal with people who are honest.

In business, honesty is absolutely essential. I find, continually, not only in my consultancy work, but in my public customer care courses, that many people make promises they cannot keep. For example, they promise the delivery of an order in a week, but it takes three weeks. The best principle is 'under-promise and over-deliver'.

We can all have difficulties with the bluntness of honest people, but there is security in knowing where you stand. In my management programmes, I stress to managers how important it is that they are truthful. It can appear that one is being cruel, but there are occasions when one has to be cruel to be kind. For example, it could be that a manager is criticizing another person's appearance, but the honesty behind this means that the recipient of the criticism will be the beneficiary in the long term.

Moral courage

Telling the truth takes moral courage, and it is great to see people who have it. You always know where you are with that person and you know you can trust them. We sometimes call this 'strength of personality'.

It is equally important not to exaggerate. I find it so frustrating that some people will exaggerate either to impress or to make a story that's anyway good even more of an attention grabber. In business and in relationships, it is so dangerous to give incorrect information. Over-exaggerated or even under-exaggerated information can prompt others to make entirely the wrong decisions.

We can only aspire to greater achievement and success if we have accurate information to rely on. I regularly ask managers, 'What sort of manager would you like to be managed by?'

Try asking yourself that question, and also think about the following: 'What sort of parent would you like to have?', 'What sort of brother or sister would you like to have?', 'What sort of partner would you like to have?', 'What sort of boyfriend or girlfriend would you like to have?' Now ask yourself: 'AM I THAT SORT OF PERSON?'

How to build a success attitude

I keep emphasizing how important the success attitude is; so let us see how to achieve it.

1. Expect the best

This is the foundation of positive thinking. It is how you mentally approach every day, month and year. Is it with positive thoughts or negative thoughts? When you look at your post, do you expect good news or bad news? If somebody says there is an urgent phone call, is your reaction 'What's gone wrong, am I in trouble, is there a crisis?' or do you think, 'Oh good! I'm expecting some good news.'

Of course, occasionally you will have a frustrating phone call, you will occasionally get something in the post that can be a bit of a shock and, realistically, you will from time to time have a bad day, but these should be *exceptions* to the rule.

Build your 'success attitude' by always having a positive attitude: expect good news, expect each day to be a wonderful, fun day. It is truly amazing how the interruptions to your enjoyment become fewer and fewer.

2. Make it a habit to be positive

Most habits take a little while to cultivate and transform into subconscious, automatic behaviour. Normally, when we talk about a habit, it is in a negative context: the habits of smoking, drinking, biting one's nails, etc. There are other habits that relate to thought and communication, such as:

- 'I make it a habit not to smile.'
- 'I make it a habit not to show my emotions.'
- 'I can't stop myself worrying, I'm always expecting the worst.'

These are all examples of activity and thought made into a habit by repetition. So, how about making it a habit to be positive, to be happy, to enjoy every day, and how about making it a habit to avoid some of the negative thoughts that damage your own self-image?

3. Use repetition to change your attitude

If you accept that you can be habitually positive, that will be the end result. To achieve that, you must actively use the principle of repetition.

Athletes build muscle by continual repetition. The strongest men in the world have built phenomenal strength by the continual development of their muscles. Every day, they spend long hours repetitively pumping their muscles into and then beyond the pain threshold. Although the brain is not a muscle, it will respond like a muscle to repetition.

I have already given numerous examples of the importance of continually giving the right messages to the brain. I believe that 10 repetitions of a thought will create the foundation upon which the skyscraper of positivity will stand.

I believe we can all change our attitudes as long as we understand what attitude is and can distinguish between positive and negative thought patterns. To those who claim attitudes cannot be changed, I reply that I have seen over the years the most wonderful achievements made by people who have changed from having a negative to having a positive attitude, a change brought on by simply being exposed to the messages I have included in this book. Nobody is born into this world negative; we are born with a positive attitude, but are conditioned to be negative.

4. Smile

Make it a habit to smile – this is probably terribly corny and rather basic, but you will find it so much harder to have negative thoughts when you are smiling. If you consciously change your facial expression, somehow the movement of muscles into a smile reflects back into the brain, and negative thoughts can seem to be replaced by something much more positive.

My great mentor as a speaker and communicator, Peter Riggs, used to claim that as a lazy person, he took up smiling because he understood that we use fewer muscles smiling than we do frowning. He claimed this was the reason why his most wonderful face was a bit like a wrinkled prune!

Smile as you wake in the morning – if you share your bed with anybody else, you will be amazed by the response! Smile as you go to work – people may look away initially, but it is so infectious that they will not be able to resist the temptation to have another look at a smiling face. Smile at your colleagues. Think how much nicer it is to talk to or be in the company of a person with a smiling and happy face.

5. Try not to burden other people

Of course, we all share some of our burdens or worries with those we are close to. Occasionally, sharing a problem with somebody else can lessen the pressure. A joy that is shared is a joy that is doubled; a problem that is shared can be a problem halved.

Betty Rice-Hunt was 63 when she lost her husband, Alva, to cancer. After his death she devoted some of her time raising money for cancer research. She kept a very active social life as well as time for her family. Latterly, she experienced enormous pain from osteoporosis and various other ailments, but she never ceased her fund-raising activities. At the age of 84 she was presented with a certificate by Sir Angus Ogilvy for raising the highest sum ever by an individual for the Imperial Cancer Research Fund.

The reason I tell this story is that even though Betty experienced enormous pain and discomfort, could no longer drive her car and had great difficulty even moving around, she was always positive and made a habit of not burdening other people with her health problems. The consequence was that it was always a joy to spend time with her, or chat to her on the phone. She was a great example of someone with a success attitude.

6. Plan on doing something positive each day

'Positive actions equal positive results.' That principle obviously leads to positive thought. But by planning and doing something each day that is constructive, you will progress towards your goal. One of the laws of motivation states that seeing ourselves progressing motivates us. Again, a motivated brain is positive and exhibits the 'success attitude'.

7. Be honest

By being honest with other people and with yourself, you will become more self-assured and more confident. Honesty with yourself allows you to know where you are and what you believe. Honesty with others enables them to know where you and they stand.

8. Discard negative thoughts

If happiness is determined by your mental outlook, it therefore seems vital to discard thoughts that make you unhappy. Easily done, first by simply determining not to think in this way, and secondly, by replacing those negative thoughts with positive thoughts.

When you have had a film developed and you see your photographs printed, you normally discard those that are out of focus, or where the lighting was wrong, as you wish to keep only the quality images. Your mind works in the same way. Cast out the negative images and replace them with positive images.

9. Think of 'problems' as challenges

How about a life with no more problems? I have asked this question of many audiences over the years and have always had an enthusiastic, positive response: 'Oh, wouldn't life be so much better without problems.' Well, there is one place where I can guarantee that the residents have no problems and that, of course, is the graveyard. If that is so, problems must be a hazard of life. Could it be possible, then, that the more alive and active we are, the more problems we encounter? If so, try to avoid using the word 'problem' and endeavour to call it a 'challenge'. Yes, of course it sounds a little bit simple and it may not make the situation go away, but your mind positively embraces a 'challenge', whereas a problem is such a demotivator.

In Chinese, the word *wei-chi,* literally translated, means 'crisis' and 'danger'. The same characters together also mean 'opportunity'.

10. Managing change

More change has taken place in the last 40 years than in the whole history of humankind. For your lifetime and mine, change will be with us. You can view it as a threat or an opportunity, but you cannot stop it. It is no good hoping it will go away, or nostalgically looking back wishing to bring back the 'good ol' days'. Most change actually turns out positively, but we fear change because it brings uncertainty. Are we going to be worse off? Can we meet this new challenge or expectation? Will we be able to cope? Your brain is fantastic and it will and it can. Give it the chance. Thousands, possibly millions, of people in the 1990s learnt how to use a computer for the first time. So embrace change positively, enthusiastically; see what might be and not what was.

As a final thought, accept the saying 'I can alter my life by altering the attitude of my mind.'

Pocket Reminders

- Expect the best
- Make it a habit to be positive
- Use repetition to change your attitude
- Remember to smile (do it now!)
- Try not to burden other people
- Plan on doing something positive each day
- Be honest with yourself and others
- Discard negative thoughts
- Think of 'problems' as 'challenges'
- Managing change.

WISE WORDS

Kind words can be short and easy to speak, but their echoes are truly endless.

Mother Theresa

11

Overcoming Setbacks

It is all very well being positive, but we also need to be realistic. Life is not one straightforward steady climb to a pinnacle of success. We all have our ups and downs, our pleasures and sorrows, our successes and failures. Most of us are extremely able to cope when things are going well, when there are no problems at home, when all is well at work, the bills are being paid, the bank is happy and goals are steadily being achieved.

Most of us do not have to learn how to cope with the successes of life, although there are situations when people achieve dramatic success and this does indeed change their behaviour. There are occasions when people have to learn how to cope with sudden or dramatic success. The consequences if they do not may mean that they are ostracized by their immediate family connections and friends, and this of course is sad and unnecessary.

This chapter is about how to manage the times of crisis, disaster or failure as well as setbacks, fears, worries and anything else that can be a barrier to our success.

We are able to manage and then overcome those downturns in order to be able to be a true positive thinker and to be able to master life with all the opportunities and joys that are available.

Everybody, whoever they are, whatever they have done and achieved, has experienced and will experience from time to time a fear, a worry or a setback. The only place where one does not have a fear or a worry to cope with is a graveyard. I remember saying this at one of my lectures, and a wise comedian shouted out from the audience, 'If that is so, maybe the worries and fears we have are a sign that we are really living?' Perhaps you and I are really living when we have lots to cope with.

DEMOTIVATORS

These setbacks, fears and worries are, in most cases, de-motivators and it makes sense to try to prevent ourselves from becoming demotivated. What causes you to be de-motivated? Having clearly identified the causes, it is logical to do everything you possibly can to gradually eliminate them. Note that the demotivators are separate from our fears and worries and setbacks.

If you are demotivated, or your attitude is in a rut, you will be unable to make the right decisions or exert influence over others. The only difference between a rut and a grave is how long you keep working at it!

We will start by examining some of the emotions which can be barriers to our success, then we will look at how to handle them positively and overcome them.

CAUSES OF UNHAPPINESS

Prior to looking at how we can build and maintain the 'success attitude', let's examine a few human characteristics that make people feel unhappy. Unhappiness, of course, can lead to depression and it is a bit like a barometer – when it falls, stormy conditions can be expected.

Envy

Envy destroys the human heart and soul, and most who suffer from it are unaware of the destructive misery it creates not only for themselves, but also for others. In the end, envy will lead to loneliness as other people can never share their joys, successes or happiness with an envious person. In addition, an envious person uses up so much of their mental energy in negative, destructive thought, denigrating other people's achievements as dishonest, harmful or detrimental.

Bitterness and revenge

Bitterness and revenge are, of course, two different emotions, but nevertheless, one seems to feed the other in many instances. Both of these characteristics, in so many cases, deal with past events. Unfortunate past events should be left in the history books rather than be allowed to cause mental turmoil and negative thoughts. If it is consigned to the history book, we can do absolutely nothing about it, other than learn from the experience to avoid making the same mistakes again.

Revenge is wasteful as it can use up productive and creative thought. If that same creative energy and time were directed positively, the outcome would be success. If everybody followed the doctrine of an eye for an eye, the world would eventually become blind. This may sound rather pious and there are, of course, times when it is very difficult and maybe even wrong to turn the other cheek. What I am stressing is that we cannot be successful if our minds are twisted with bitterness and revenge.

Depression

Mild depression is in most cases within one's control. I mentioned it briefly in Chapter 10 – The Success Attitude, but it is worth reiterating that we cannot possibly be successful if we are suffering from depression. The causes can be so varied, and those who truly want to manage this condition will be well advised to begin by seeking the cause, the spark that lights this unfortunate fire, and then systematically taking steps to make sure that the spark is not lit: in other words, ruthlessly preventing the situations that cause depressed feelings. Regular exercise has proved to be one of the best antidotes to depression. A good walk, workout in the gym, bike ride or swim is so effective. More serious depression, of course, requires expert medical treatment and counselling, and in these cases it is no good telling a depressed person to 'snap out of it'.

Bereavement

We all accept that the loss of a loved one is a cause of great unhappiness and I am not going to be so facetious or disrespectful as to suggest some glib, instantaneous technique for turning this situation into a happy experience. The success attitude is no defence to experiencing sadness as well as joy and pleasure.

If one does lose a loved one, through either death or the breakdown of a relationship, time, as we are always told, is a great healer. I can guarantee that you must have faith. But equally, it is not right to allow ourselves to wallow in our misery to such an extent that we make other people miserable. It takes positive effort and determination to stop thinking about something one can no longer do anything about and to turn our thoughts to the future. With a determined effort, try to make other people happy and, in turn, the burden will become a little lighter.

Crime and guilt

Our prisons and places of confinement are inhabited by people who have committed offences against society. These institutions are not happy places. The vast majority of the inmates, through lack of self-management, control or willpower, had believed that by taking the risk and committing a crime against society, they would somehow achieve happiness by their actions. Sadly, the opposite is true. Whatever the crime that may have been committed, the biggest theft of all is from themselves: their liberty and their life. There can be very little pleasure in gains made by unsociable behaviour. People who commit crime are generally unhappy, and even those who are not institutionalized have to live with the fear that one day their activities will be discovered. They are also ensnared by their own poor self-image and guilt.

Family problems

If you are fortunate enough to be part of a family, of course you are going to face difficult situations, challenges and opportunities. If approached with love, care and responsibility, and without any selfish thought or action, families can bring great joy and security.

The penultimate chapter of this book will deal in more detail with the great joy and happiness that is available for any of us fortunate enough to share our lives with another person.

Our own unhappiness

If we think about ourselves in a negative, dissatisfied way, of course we become unhappy. If we look at ourselves in the mirror and we are dreadfully unhappy with what we see, if our thought processes are continually self-destructive and we do not see the goodness within ourselves, unhappiness and dissatisfaction are unavoidable.

You need, if you are at all unhappy, to concentrate on your positive attributes and to dedicate your energies to actively building a 'success attitude'.

OVERCOMING SETBACKS

'Prevention is better than cure': but anybody who does anything in the world experiences setbacks, and the more things you do, the more likely it is that you will experience setbacks.

Mistakes

Some people are so fearful of making a mistake that they do nothing, or try nothing new, and the consequence is that they achieve very little. It is perfectly acceptable to make mistakes occasionally – it is a sign of activity. We all learn more from our mistakes than from our achievements.

But it is very stupid to continue making the same mistake over and over again. Setbacks can be the result of a mistake, or they can be the result of situations that we find ourselves in, perhaps even through no fault of our own.

I recall the very first major setback I experienced in my working career.

I had a small farm in the south of England. About 7 miles from our main farm was some 40 acres of land where I was the tenant. This land was essential, as I used it primarily for cutting and making hay to feed my livestock in the winter. One year, in May, prior to haymaking in June, I was notified that I had to give up the land immediately. The reasons why are unimportant, but I had no legal right to stay.

For me, this was a crisis of monumental proportions; without this land the farm could not survive. I did not have sufficient fodder for the next winter, I was unable to borrow any further money from the bank, and to find available land to rent at that time of the year would be impossible, or so I thought.

I suppose I did what anyone would do, and that was to become extremely worried and depressed. I felt I had no future, no way out and I was going to go broke. I did not keep my worries to myself, but shared them with the family. However, a very good friend quoted a saying that I have never forgotten, and it turned this setback into another opportunity: 'In every adversity there is the seed of an equivalent or greater benefit.' He went on to say, 'Do something about it and stop wallowing in your own self-pity.'

Well, I did. I picked up the phone and contacted all my farming connections. I got in the car and visited people, and within a few days, by a 'stroke of luck', I came across another piece of land. The acreage was not exactly the same, but it was very similar. It was only a mile and a half away and the rent was a little less than I had previously been paying. We all said, 'It's worked out for the best in the end.'

Now, you must have had a similar experience in your life, where you have been faced with a crisis or a setback and consciously or subconsciously, having come through the first few days of misery and self-pity, you turned the setback around. It is a mistake you will not make again. It can be the experience from which you develop a philosophy and it can turn into a situation where you really are better off than before.

Turn setbacks to your advantage

So, whenever you are faced with those hurdles or barriers, setbacks or crises, say to yourself, **'How can I turn this to my advantage?'** Just asking yourself that one question will switch your thought processes from negative to positive.

Throughout this book, the concepts and ideas for achievement and success revolve around our thought processes. It is quite extraordinary in the world, how when the world's leaders are in positive thought mode, economies grow, jobs are created and the threat of world conflict is reduced.

Natalie du Toit, the South African paralympic swimmer who won four gold medals at Athens in 2004, was knocked off her scooter when returning from training in February 2001. Her left leg was amputated just below the knee and her Olympic dream was over. She switched her attention to the Athens Paralympics. She says, 'I'm one of those people who can truthfully say, out of something bad came something good. The tragedy of life doesn't lie in not reaching your goal, the tragedy lies in having no goal to reach.' She goes on to say, 'It isn't a calamity to die with dreams unfulfilled but it is a calamity not to dream. It isn't a disgrace not to reach the stars, but it is a disgrace to have no stars to reach for.'

SITUATIONS AND CHALLENGES

'Problem' is such a negative word. If you tell yourself you have a problem, you normally dwell on it and worry about it. If, instead, you delete the word 'problem' from your vocabulary and use the words 'situation' or 'challenge', your brain will respond more effectively. It becomes creative and proactive and, furthermore, you are on your way to overcoming the situation. Remember the old cliché 'When the going gets tough, the tough get going.'

Having a system or methodology for handling setbacks, only allowing yourself a short period to worry before looking for solutions, allows you to take positive action and turn it to your advantage.

OVERCOMING FEARS

There are some things it is perfectly rational to fear – drugs, drinking poison, falling over a cliff – situations in which your body is in imminent danger, but these are not the fears that we need to concentrate on overcoming. What are you afraid of? This is very personal as one person's fear is not necessarily another's. Realistically, everybody is afraid of something. Here are a few common fears:

- death;
- poverty;
- failure;
- ill health;
- old age;
- rejection;
- loss of love;
- mistakes;
- success;
- being laughed at;
- being criticized.

One can be even more specific:

- public speaking;
- riding a horse;

- skiing;
- swimming;
- meeting people;
- driving a car;
- flying in an aeroplane.

And there are, of course, the phobias that some people experience, ie: 'I'm terrified of spiders/snakes/rats.' As this is such a huge subject I will not deal with it here. I want to concentrate on overcoming unnecessary fears. In many cases, fear can be a stimulant and can be used to our advantage.

Fear of failure

Once again, as with nearly all human emotions, there is a balance and it must be managed. In my book *Motivate to Win*, I said, 'Don't ever fear failure.' And, for years, I truly believed that it was a weakness to fear failure. My eldest son, Lyster, debated this very subject with me one day and he said, 'I have to disagree with you. The fear of failure has been one of my greatest motivators. Just the thought of failing has driven me and helped my business to grow.'

As a result, I have modified my opinion. There is nothing wrong with the fear of failure; it is the visualization of failure that is so damaging. When you continually visualize the failure scenario, it will almost inevitably create the result.

I said that fear could be a great stimulant or motivator. We can see this in the animal kingdom. Fear keeps wild animals alive. In the wild, every animal is alert, fearing the predator; the slightest movement or unusual sound causes instant flight. As a human, we will run faster or jump higher if we are frightened.

So, fear can be managed if used positively, but for the majority of us, to overcome a fear we need to find and then be able to use a guaranteed, workable system. We usually have only one or two fears which we will not risk exposing, yet at the same time we would dearly love to overcome them.

Managing fear

The best way of overcoming a fear is to keep doing the thing you fear to do. We all know this to be true and all it takes is that first step, that first little bit of courage. It is quite extraordinary how, once we have participated in an activity that has previously been a fear, our confidence grows and how much easier it is the next time, until what used to be a fear is just an everyday part of life. Fear is an imagination, not a reality. It is only the thought of what might happen that creates fear.

When we finally summon up the courage to tackle a fear or a problem head on, it somehow disappears. You know the sort of thing: making that difficult phone call, giving somebody a ticking off, or perhaps even firing an employee. One wakes up at night, worrying 'What am I going to say?' Continually thinking about the dreaded event can be more painful than actually doing it.

That difficult phone call is rarely as bad as we thought it was going to be. Sometimes when you have to fire someone, you may find they are actually quite relieved and were about to go anyhow. We all have our fears, for whatever reason, but if we truly want to overcome them, we can – and what a marvellous achievement overcoming a fear really is.

DEALING WITH WORRY

What is a worry? The word is derived from the Anglo-Saxon *wyrgan*, which means to strangle. A modern understanding of the word would describe it as a disturbed state of mind, or allowing one's mind to dwell on difficulties or trouble. Worrying really is the negative use of our brain's imagination. Worrying about what might happen in the future or dwelling on the possible ramifications of a situation that has already occurred is negative visualization. The quotation 'What you fear may come upon you' has already been discussed and, unfortunately, is too accurate to be dismissed. Henry Ford stated, 'If you think you can, or you think you can't, you are right.' Unfortunately, some people spend so much time worrying and negatively visualizing that their vision is fulfilled.

Here are some of the expressions that people voice while in this state of worry:

- 'I'm so worried I can't think straight.'
- 'I'm so worried I can't sleep.'
- 'I'm worried to death.'
- 'I'm so worried there is nothing I can do.'
- 'I'm so worried I can't get over what happened to me.'
- 'I'm so worried I'll get it wrong.'

When we look at these in black and white, it seems ridiculous to allow ourselves to voice these expressions. Though it is natural and understandable to do so, we must accept that worries are a disturbed state of mind, they are negative visualizations, they can be the cause of more fears, they create depression; and that all of these can eventually lead to ill health, unhappiness, misery, frustration, desperation and, in the worst-case scenario, even suicide.

Worries must be confronted. We all experience them to various degrees, but they can and must be managed. First of all, remember 'a worry shared is a worry halved; a joy that is shared is a joy that is doubled'. But by sharing a worry we do, of course, run the risk that a loved one or a colleague may also become worried. On the other hand, though, it may be the first stage towards a solution.

We must also accept that the vast majority of situations that we worry about never actually come about. I have found that the two most effective ways to deal with a worry are first, never to allow myself to worry about what *might* happen, and secondly, to write down my fears and worries.

Worrying about what *might* happen

I find the easiest way is to imagine the worst scenario that could happen. In those circumstances, what would I do? How would I handle it? I then formulate in my mind a plan for handling the situation and, having prepared a plan of action in my mind, I can delete that worry and I do not think about it again. In most cases you will find that if you follow that simple procedure the worry will disappear as all your thought processes are concentrating on positive action.

When you brainstorm ideas, you often find solutions to a worry – this is really a 'positive thinker's' habit. But to continually visualize a worry scenario is perhaps what *wyrgan* means: 'to strangle, to choke until there is no life left'.

Writing down your worries

You may find it helpful to write your worries or fears down on a piece of paper. When they are written down, they never seem as bad as when you are mulling them over in your mind.

There is another great little system that works well for some people – to have a 'worry box'. It is a little bit like a piggybank, and what you do as soon as you have a worry is to write it down on a piece of paper and put it in the 'worry box' and then, at the end of the month, empty it out with the family. You will find that not only have the majority somehow been solved, but many of the items have become a bit of a laugh rather than a worry.

I can assure you, it is very effective. From now on, whenever you are worried, do something.

If you wish to achieve your goals, I really must stress that any time spent worrying will be an inhibitor. Worrying achieves absolutely nothing other than depression and stress, so endeavour not to do it.

So there is the message: if you have a worry, do something, take action, be positive; do not let it fester.

Pocket Reminders

- Identify your demotivators and gradually eliminate them

- Turn setbacks to your advantage

- Change the word 'problem' to 'situation' or 'challenge'

- Let fear be a stimulant

- Be positive with worries – write them down, or use a 'worry box'

- Worrying is an inhibitor of success, so take action and be positive.

WISE WORDS

Failure is not in failing: it's in not trying.

Stella James

12

Mastering Rejection

Rejection is normally expressed by a silly little word – No. Written down, it looks fairly harmless and hardly daunting, but the truth is that this simple word can stop you from achieving your goals. Unless you are truly able to deal with it, it will restrict your future progress.

OVERCOMING REJECTION

Rejection is, for many of us, difficult to overcome. When we were children, the word 'No' was used as a form of control: 'No, don't touch', 'No, don't step off the pavement', 'No, don't put your hand in the fire', and, as a result, we became more and more conditioned to the word 'No' preventing us from doing what we wanted – although it often stopped us from getting hurt.

Fear of the word 'no'

From our very early years, both our subconscious and our conscious minds process the word 'no' as a safety mechanism.

For example, a young man who wants to ask a girl for a date is so fearful that she might say 'No' that he does not even ask.

Why is it that people seeking a job are happier to write lots of letters in the hope of getting an interview than to pick up the phone and ask, or go and make a visit? The worst that can happen is that an employer will say, 'No, I don't have a vacancy', 'No, the time is not right' or, perhaps, 'No, you're not what we are looking for'. Let us look at some more scenarios.

- Individuals who really believe that their working conditions or remuneration are unfair do not always ask to have them changed. Why?
- Many people fill in coupons to borrow money, in most cases at almost double the interest and repayment rate, rather than visit a bank because they fear a 'No'.

There is a very common reaction among the vast majority of the population, who claim they could never be any good at selling. They feel they would be unable to cope with rejection, with somebody saying, 'No, thank you.'

Success, as I have repeatedly said, is available to you and this may mean doing things differently – grasping challenges, establishing relationships – and undoubtedly you are going to be confronted with many situations where people have a choice and they can say 'No'.

Another way of looking at the word 'no'

First, let us truly understand what 'No' means. It is not a rejection of *you* in 99 per cent of cases – and so what if it is anyhow?

This book is about the real world. I have heard lecturers propounding the idea that every time a salesperson gets a 'No', he or she is one step closer to a 'Yes'. That may be statistically correct, but it still does not mean that we are ever going to enjoy people saying 'No' to us.

I have personally found that the most effective way to deal with the word 'No' is to understand that 'No' is only 'No' at that point in time. It does not mean 'No' next week, next month or next year.

I can guarantee that you have purchased something, been somewhere or done something in the last few months that previously you said 'No' to. The reason is that your circumstances will have changed. You may have the funds, the opportunity, or more time, which means that you now buy or do what you had previously refused to buy or do.

In my business career, I can look back and see the times when I have attempted to do a business deal and have received a 'No thank you, not suitable, time not right', etc. With a little persistence, and by keeping in contact, that 'No' can eventually be turned round to a 'Yes'.

Asking does not hurt

We have all overheard people saying, 'I just don't like asking people for anything.' Sometimes this is because that person fears being rejected or perhaps it is because they do not like being obligated or in debt to another person.

However, you must realize that asking will not hurt you and, equally, understand that some people just yearn to be asked. They are fearful of wanting to appear to impose, they are shy, they do not want to interfere and some, equally, are fearful of offering because they might be rejected. Most successful people ask if they want something done or they require information.

Now just suppose 50 per cent of the time you ask you get a 'No'. That means 50 per cent of the time you are going to be better off, you are going to get help and it may also help others – and, let me remind you, it is impossible not to be successful if you make others successful.

So, do not be a martyr – you cannot be successful without help from others.

Taking 'no' personally

So, do not ever take a 'no' personally, do not take it as a rejection – it is not a failure, it is just an unsatisfactory result at that particular moment.

Persistence

One of the most powerful ingredients of success is persistence. A sales manager once told me that the greatest quality he looked for in his staff was the ability to persist. A person who is able to persist – and yes, you can too – will eventually prevail and win.

It does not matter what the challenge or opportunity is. If you are prepared to keep tapping away at it, you will succeed in the end.

Could you knock a six-inch nail into a seasoned piece of oak with one hit? Of course not, but a child could drive that nail in, perhaps even with a wooden hammer, with a sufficient number of taps, over a sufficient period of time.

The opposite of persistence is giving up, and this appears to be the norm for many people. Statistically, it is shown that most people quit:

- within two weeks of starting a keep-fit programme;

- within four days of starting a diet;
- within eight months of starting a savings plan.

> My company sales manager called on a major high street bank to see if the trainers would like to buy some of our videos and services, but they declined the offer. So he asked if he could keep in contact and see them again in six months' time and they agreed. Six months later, again they declined, but nevertheless, he and I had built a bit of a relationship with the people at the bank. Six months later we discovered that the decision makers had moved on and we had to start all over again.
>
> Well, every six months, we had meetings followed by 'No thank you', and again the people who we thought we had built a relationship with were moved on. At last, four years later, they gave us a trial on two videos and then a further order came in.
>
> Six months later, an order for £50,000 worth of videos was received. One year later, this increased to £80,000 worth of videos and other products. The following year we were able to supply a quarter of a million pounds worth of business to this one client.

Giving up

Try not to let giving up become a habit. Every invention that we now take for granted in our personal lives is the result of persistence. Edison made thousands of attempts to produce a light bulb; Fleming's discovery of penicillin was due to persistence. There are now drugs that not only control but, in some cases, cure cancer. Once again, this is due to persistence.

The list is endless, but all have been achieved through hundreds or even thousands of attempts and by getting it wrong until a solution was found.

So, persistence is a winning ingredient. There is, however, a balance between knowing when to quit and when to be stubborn. You may absolutely hate your job or your environment and just stubbornly persist in being unhappy. There is a difference in being stubborn and being persistent, but most of us seem to give up too early.

> A few years ago, during the Fastnet Race, a number of yachts were caught in storms and many people lost their lives. It was subsequently discovered that those who had left their yachts too early and taken to the lifeboats were the ones who died. If they had only stayed with their yachts, they would be alive today. Yes, there is a time to leave the ship, and that is, of course, when your feet are in the water.

The skill is to be totally honest with yourself. Being stubborn is a destructive trait and is therefore negative and normally requires little action to change. Being persistent is being positive, attempting some new action or a new approach. When you have run out of the new, or are spending too much time trying to salvage, this is the time to stop. You must have found how, when things look really extraordinarily bleak, they take a turn for the better. All successful people have experienced this – when the temptation to give up is so strong, and then suddenly everything seems to come right. I have heard people describe this as the eleventh hour principle so, once again, do not give in; you may just be experiencing the eleventh hour principle.

If you want something, whatever it may be, persist – persistence will master virtually any rejection.

Accept that there is absolutely nothing wrong in asking. If we look back at our life's experiences, the only things we truly regret are the things that we have not done, or did not ask for – we very rarely regret actions that we took.

So, there is no logic in fearing rejection. It must come back to those pillars of pain and pleasure, where the pain is caused by somebody saying 'No' and this outweighs the pleasure that would result if they were to say 'Yes'. Take the actions that I discussed earlier. I find it very helpful to say to myself, 'So what if they say no?'

By mastering rejection, you will be more willing and more prepared to do the things you have feared doing, because you will feel that much stronger. Whatever you do, do not visualize a negative result, do not visualize other people saying 'No' – reverse that picture in your mind.

Pocket Reminders

- Convince yourself that there is no such thing as rejection
- Remember that 'no' is only a 'no, not today'
- Do not take 'no' personally
- Ask for things: you cannot be successful without the help of others
- Be persistent and avoid giving up, but know when to quit
- Master rejection – do not let it master you.

WISE WORDS

Nothing in the world can take the place of persistence. Talent will not; nothing is more common than unsuccessful men with talent. Genius will not; unrewarded genius is almost a proverb. Education will not; the world is full of educated derelicts. Persistence and determination alone are omnipotent. The slogan 'press on' has solved and always will solve the problems of the human race.

Calvin Coolidge

13

Negativity: The Success Destroyer

This book is all about success, but now comes the hazard warning – negativity destroys success. Ignore the message from this chapter at your peril.

The success destroyer has to be a major disease of the world today. It is a total destroyer of happiness, and actual and potential success. It is a destroyer of relationships and achievements. The disease I describe is the power of the negative and it manifests itself in negative thinking, which in turn leads to negative communication.

HOW DO WE BECOME NEGATIVE?

We were all born positive, but conditioned to be negative. We discussed in Chapter 12 – Mastering Rejection, how influential the word 'no' is in all our daily lives. Our brains store the context in which the word 'no' was used in our early years, so it almost becomes a word of fear. But 'no' is not a negative word, even though the majority of us react as if it is. So, how do we become conditioned to be negative?

An easy place to start is, of course, the media – newspapers, television and radio. Journalists earn their living by finding and reporting bad news, to such an extent that if there is not sufficient they try to create it.

If we are continually bombarded with bad news, is it any wonder that so many people are negative? Is it any wonder that so many people enjoying extraordinarily high living standards in the Western world, with so much pleasure and happiness available to them, are depressed? It is so easy to expect bad news, and to some extent it creates a thirst resulting in even more being demanded.

We all know that if the newspapers feature a dreadful murder, their sales increase. The vast majority of people in the Western world have so much to look forward to, have so much protection and care provided by the state, have so much that is good, yet they feel so short-changed by their governments. So few people are really looking forward to the future. They have become conditioned by this negative process.

THE DANGERS OF NEGATIVITY

Why is negativity so dangerous? First, because it is so difficult to get rid of and also extremely expensive, as you will see. It drags us down emotionally, physically and mentally. It is, I repeat, the single biggest destroyer of success and potential success.

Negative thinking destroys relationships, creativity and achievement and, ultimately, happiness. Perhaps even more frightening, negative thinking creates the right environment for illness to grow and prosper. We attract what we fear. The more one thinks about a potential illness, the more one concentrates one's thoughts about catching a particular disease, the more one imagines one has a serious complaint when only a minor symptom is exhibited, the more likely one will be to develop that particular form of ill health. It is common sense, but nevertheless worth stating, that the more one is a positive thinker, the more likely one is to remain healthy.

Negative thinking and communication

For many people, negative thinking and communication has become a bad habit that can even be addictive. So, what is it about negativity that is so bad? It affects what people say and think to themselves. I said earlier that the poorer a person's self-image, the more negative they are likely to be, creating a vicious circle.

The habit of negative thinking

These are some of the common phrases that people often say to themselves. To be realistic, every one of us can identify with some of these, but they are examples of the thoughts and phrases that have held us back from achieving the success that is available to us.

- 'I'm too old to change now.'
- 'I'm too young.'
- 'I know I can't.'
- 'I will never be able to...'
- 'I hate doing this.'
- 'I'm just not cut out to...'
- 'I bet I catch your cold.'
- 'I'm sure I'm going to miss the train.'
- 'I'm always carsick.'
- 'I always fall off.'
- 'I'm always broke.'

- 'I've got a terrible memory.'
- 'I can't speak in public.'
- 'I'm sure that won't work.'
- 'I bet they say no.'
- 'I've got no willpower.'
- 'I'm just not clever enough.'

The list is endless.

Negative thought is a destructive use of our creative imagination. We expect the worst or we anticipate something we don't want to happen to us. It can be the total fear of rejection that we have already discussed. We imagine somebody saying 'no' to us before we have even asked. This negative fear manifests itself after every news tragedy: after a rail crash people are fearful to travel by train, after the tragedy of 9/11 (11 September 2001) world airlines experienced a dramatic downturn in passenger traffic, and the elderly are fearful in their homes each time a crime on an old person is reported.

In fact, the opposite to all this is true: the elderly are the safest members of our community and air and rail travel are hundreds of times safer than travelling by car. There are many people who at the slightest twinge in their body fear they are going to experience some dreadful illness. Our imagination, as we have already learnt, is so powerful. Do not ever let your brain or your thoughts think about something nasty happening to you. The chances are 99.9 per cent that it won't, but the damage the negative thought does to you and your relationships is beyond measure. Human conflict is littered with someone imagining their partner or their opponent is doing or is going to do something nasty to them, and all it does is create strife and more misery. In almost every section of this book, I have stressed the importance of repeating positive affirmations. Why on earth do we waste time talking or thinking about what we do not want?

DEALING WITH NEGATIVE COMMUNICATION

This particular section is not so much about what you think as about how you process what is said to you by others and how you handle negative communication in all its forms. Let us look at the three Cs:

■ Criticizing;
■ Condemning; and
■ Complaining.

Criticism

Of course, there has to be a place for constructive criticism, but a lot of criticism is not constructive; rather, it is destructive. None of us will ever grow and improve without some constructive help, but too much criticism is not constructive. Anyone can find fault. If only people would use their brilliant minds to solve problems and find better ways of doing things instead of saying, 'That won't work', 'That's a lousy idea', 'You can't do that', etc.

Condemning and complaining

Have you noticed how the media – television, radio and newspapers – have become more and more negative over the past few years? Whoever is being interviewed on whatever programme, it seems the interview has got to take the form of a conflict and the interviewer has got to play an aggressive game of devil's advocate. Whatever good idea any politician does have (and they do have some), it somehow has to be debunked and shredded. It seems that even on the phone-in programmes, all we hear is criticism, condemnation and complaint. Avoid mixing with people whose only conversation consists of the three Cs.

Living in a negative environment

I am truly amazed when I work with young people. When I start to tell them the truth about life, that it is possible to be successful and that achievements are there for the taking, their facial expressions are a delight to see: they radiate sheer exuberance and enthusiasm when the seeds of positive communication are planted. Why does our society have to destroy every new idea? Why are so many people cynical and sceptical?

The law of conformity states that as human beings we naturally conform to our environment, whatever that environment may be. So is it any wonder that if the environment is negative, people will become negative themselves?

Here is a challenge. See if you can draw up a list of really successful, but extremely negative people. I do not think you will run out of ink! Negative people are not the benchmark of success or happiness. When you visit cities throughout the world, you cannot help but notice statues erected to famous people, for their endeavours, achievements, creativity and courage. Have you ever seen a monument erected for a critic? Monuments are erected not to those who criticize, but to those who have been criticized.

Dealing with the past

If something has happened, it is now in the past. Do not use it as an excuse for misery and unhappiness, which, in turn, can be passed on to others. I cannot stress strongly enough the importance of positive rather than negative affirmations, and if there is only one message that you take from this book, this should be it.

TAKE PRECAUTIONS AGAINST NEGATIVITY

Let us look at some examples of how we respond to situations:

In hot countries, we take precautions to avoid being bitten by mosquitos. Why? Because it is painful and we risk catching malaria. So, we arm ourselves with an insect-killer and a mosquito net and we might take anti-malaria tablets.

Now, if you were bitten by a mosquito, this might be painful for 24 hours or so; but negative communication from one person to another may well change that person's life, and not just for 24 hours. Sometimes it can be for days, weeks, months or even a lifetime, yet we just let it happen.

Let me give you another example. Imagine you are driving your car on a lovely, hot, sunny day. All the windows and the sun roof are open and the traffic lights change to red. Cars draw up on either side of you and from one of the cars near you a passsenger bends down, collects up all the rubbish from inside their car and throws it straight in through your window: fish and chip wrappers, cigarette packets, drink cans all land in your car – what would you do?

I suggest you would be absolutely furious and you would almost certainly leap out and hand the rubbish back with at the very least the mildly sarcastic words 'Have you dropped these?'

Why is this such a useful example? We do not like people putting rubbish in our cars, but we allow them to put it in our minds. So, be careful. People with an open mind must be even more careful, as there are others intent on filling it full of garbage.

We must, of course, distinguish between recognizing or noticing negativity and actively thinking negatively. It is perfectly sensible and realistic to recognize what could be classified as a negative action or occurrence. You might notice that your car is dirty and turn that into negative thought: 'Somebody else got this dirty,' 'Why did they do that to me?', 'Anyway, it's the roads in Britain and our terrible climate and if we lived in California our cars wouldn't get dirty', etc. Instead of letting our thought processes run riot with negativity, we should just take action and clean the car. Getting upset is negative, and doing something about whatever it is you have noticed is positive.

ELIMINATING YOUR NEGATIVITY

Here are a few steps to help you handle and, one hopes, eventually eliminate the success destroyer.

1. Check what you say to family, friends and colleagues

Is what you say positive or negative? If it is negative, you are almost certainly harming somebody else, unless you are sure you are being constructive. So, do not make negative or nasty comments – all you will be doing is harming somebody else. You are totally in control of your own verbal communication.

2. Check what you say to yourself

Are you saying positive or negative things to yourself? Imagine a missile being fired. The senders have control of it, and if it goes off course, they can press the self-destruct button and the missile will explode. Whenever you let negative thoughts enter your mind, it is as though you have just pressed the self-destruct button. You are in control of what you think. If you know those thoughts are self-destructive, actively change them and replace them with positive thoughts. Instead of saying, 'I am a bad public speaker', say, 'I am a good public speaker'. Instead of saying, 'I am always broke', say, 'I am financially secure'. Instead of saying, 'I am ill', say, 'I am well' (this is in no way meant to sound glib or to appear unsympathetic to those who have experienced ill health or an accident).

3. Avoid negative situations

As I have stated, the purpose of the body is to transport the brain, so why transport the brain into negative situations intentionally?

Every day, motorway police experience the crass stupidity of the motoring public. When dealing with an accident, they see drivers on the other carriageway slowing down to gawp and gaze with the expectation of seeing a tangled wreck and injured people, and the consequences of this behaviour are that as they slow down to stare, they pile into each other.

Now what is the good of that? Will they benefit by absorbing into their memory the sight of blood and gore and twisted, wrecked motor cars? Of course not.

Over the years, I have given advice to people who feel they can no longer cope in their particular environment. They may feel that their workplace has become unbearable with people watching their backs, or company politics, or a boss who is truly impossible to work for, etc. Let me tell you, no reward is sufficient to justify spending one's life in that negative environment. On two occasions in my life, I have walked away from extremely valuable business investments because I found the environment to be too negative, the atmosphere too unpleasant and the price just not worth paying.

4. Avoid television, video or cinema programmes that are highly negative

I am appalled by sociologists and psychiatrists who claim that 'video nasties' are not harmful and that they have not contributed to the increase in child crime or copycat murders and mass killings in the world. Like any accountant, they seem to be able to find statistics to prove anything.

Television is a wonderful medium, its primary functions being to inform and entertain. Information comes through the news and documentaries and 'lifestyle' programmes. Entertainment comes from comedies, plays, concerts, musicals, etc. I get no joy from seeing husbands beating their wives or people killing children. This, unfortunately, can be found in the news.

It has been proved that when people are continually exposed to human horror they become conditioned. In the Western world, for example, we have become numb to the sight of starving children and adults. So, if we are continually exposed to nastiness for its entertainment value, is it any wonder that standards of human relationships get lower and lower?

Every sane person with common sense knows deep down that those programmes can be powerfully influential. I personally never watch a nasty DVD, television programme or film that contains human conflict or strife. I will not watch programmes that contain marital screaming matches and brutality. I will not watch any programme that is produced for the sake of horror. My brain is too valuable to be polluted with this rubbish and, to my simple way of thinking, this can hardly be called entertainment as, unfortunately, it can be seen in the news programmes.

Some time ago, we acquired satellite television. My wife started to watch some of the late-night movies. And some of these movies were quite frightening. After several weeks, I noticed, as did she, that she was less able to cope, more depressed and much more willing to think or communicate negative thoughts and worries. We discussed what had happened in our lives to cause this change and there had been no alteration in our lives, other than her watching these programmes. She stopped, and reverted back to her normal self.

If we are honest, this should come as no surprise. If the last images we have before going to sleep are frightening or worrying, it is no wonder that the brain is in turmoil. It was born to be positive and creative.

5. Give up negative thinking

For many people, negative thinking has become a habit and many are almost addicted to bad news. If they did not want it, the media would not provide it – the press could not survive if there was no market for bad news. Now, any addiction has control over us. So, test your habit or addiction and see if you can go for, say, 12 or even 24 hours without having a negative thought. If you achieve that, fantastic! Like all habits that one wishes to break, it takes time. So, give yourself 30 days of continually avoiding negative thoughts.

HANDLING NEGATIVITY IN OTHERS

Dealing with our own negativity is one thing, but we also need to deflect the negativity of others in order to preserve our own positive thoughts. So, here are a few tips on handling others' negativity.

1. Be understanding

When somebody says something negative to you, it is ridiculous and, in many cases, uncaring to respond with some glib comment. It may be somebody very close to you: a loved one, colleague, close friend or a member of your family.

They may say something negative, voice a criticism or a complaint or a condemnation, but try to understand why it was said. Ask yourself why he or she said that. They may be feeling negative because they were worried, they may be fearful of certain consequences, or they may just be misinformed. If you are to be an effective communicator, you must learn to understand other people's feelings. You don't have to agree, but you can be very positive and optimistic and, one hopes, change their thoughts.

2. Mix with positive people

If you are in an environment where negative people are affecting you, pick up the phone and have a chat with your positive friends. Perhaps go and visit them, have a beer or a coffee with these positive people – step out of that negative environment into a positive one.

3. Be prepared to walk away

If you find yourself in a negative environment, whatever the occasion, be prepared to walk away – it just takes common sense. In any situation that you do not like, remember it is your life and your brain, and negative situations or communication can play no part whatsoever in your success or happiness. Rather than being cowardice, walking away is, I believe, more like bravery. It is more cowardly to join in, be a part of and add to the negativity.

4. Be realistic

Build your own vocabulary and understanding of what is negative. Constructive criticism is not negative, so be enthusiastic about it. Remember, you are very fortunate if you receive it. Encourage others to offer constructive criticism.

5. Do not shoot the messenger

There is always the danger of becoming so ultra-positive that you don't want to hear the bad news. Some people in authority, whether in politics or business, surround themselves with 'yes' people, but we all know they do not last for long and they are never classified as successes. The messenger or the bearer of the bad news must be welcomed. No decisions can be taken that have any chance of success unless they are based on accurate and up-to-date information.

6. Do not overreact to other people's opinions

Remember, all opinions are just that – an opinion. They can be right or wrong. As we know, we all have the human characteristic of wanting or hoping for recognition in whatever form. Previously in this chapter, I used the media as an example of negative communication. Many lives are totally destroyed by what journalists write. Even if it is fictitious, the individual is often unable to protect him- or herself from the libel. I know personally of many people who are desperately hurt by what somebody may say or think about them: a word overheard in conversation, the overheard telephone call. But one must recognize that what is said may not be real feeling, but an attempt to be interesting or amusing. And even if it is a real feeling, do not let it hurt you. Build a bulletproof screen around yourself so that other people's opinions, if negative or hurtful, cannot penetrate. Visualize your plate-glass screen of protection now.

7. Have an antidote for negative comments

Picture in your mind the most negative person you know: the one who is always griping, moaning, finding fault, criticizing and complaining, or the person who just somehow seems to be happy when they are being negative or nasty about others. Next time you meet this person and you ask them how they are (which is always a dangerous thing to ask a negative person), be ready with your antidote. Their reply in its mildest form is usually something like 'Under the circumstances, things could be worse.' Quick as a flash, you say, 'Fantastic!' The look of surprise you will receive is reward in itself but, perhaps just as importantly, the conversation will dramatically change or the individual will seek solace away from you, among the other negative people.

Pocket Reminders

- Check what you say to family, friends and colleagues
- Check what you say to yourself
- Avoid negative situations
- Do not watch negative or destructive programmes on television or DVD
- Banish negative thinking
- Be understanding of others
- Mix with positive people
- Be prepared to walk away
- Be realistic
- Do not overreact to other people's opinions
- Have an antidote for a negative comment.

WISE WORDS

Why not go out on a limb? That's where all the fruit is.

14

Irresistible Enthusiasm

It seems that every feat of human endeavour involves an enthusiast inspiring others to triumph. Every individual achieving greatness exhibits enthusiasm. So enthusiasm must therefore be one of the ingredients of success. Some cynics deride enthusiastic characteristics, but we all know how exhilarating it is to be in the company of enthusiastic people who talk passionately about a belief, a product, an idea or even an experience. 'Nothing great was ever achieved without enthusiasm,' said Ralph Waldo Emerson.

PASSION AND ENTHUSIASM

In this chapter, I will discuss passion and enthusiasm, and I am sure we can say the same about passion as we do about enthusiasm – that every success story is achieved by people with passion.

Passion and enthusiasm are two magnets that attract attention, support and participation. They also draw successful, like-minded people towards each other. They are like a bright light attracting a moth – they attract friendship, love and respect.

ENTHUSIASTIC PEOPLE

If you allow your mind to wander and think of the part enthusiasm plays in your daily life, the people you like to meet, the people you like to talk to, the people you look forward to phoning and the people you would really choose to spend your time with, I am sure, like me, you would choose those who exhibit a common characteristic – enthusiasm. Enthusiastic people are a joy to be with and their enthusiasm enhances our lives.

Would you agree that enthusiastic people seem also to be more attractive? Does enthusiasm, like motivation (which we will discuss in Chapter 15 – Self-motivation), have a certain power?

Would you agree that if you are having a party, your party will go better if you have one or two enthusiastic guests? They are the bright light, the magnet – the attraction for others.

ENTHUSIASM IS A STATE OF MIND

Enthusiasm has to be a state of mind. Perhaps it is an outward expression of our state of mind. It inspires us to action, it is contagious, inspiring not only the host, but all who come into contact. Enthusiasm is like a fuel, an extra source of energy. The great leaders throughout history have instilled and inspired passion and enthusiasm in others.

In my book *Communicate to Win*, I stress that the most vital factor in public speaking, the one that will hold an audience's attention, is for the presenter to be enthusiastic regarding his or her subject. Enthusiasm at work somehow can make a boring or mundane activity a pleasure; the time goes faster and the effort is more rewarding.

Whatever you do, enthusiasm is within your power – grasp it, work on it and see the effects.

BUILDING ENTHUSIASM

So, let us list some ideas to help you build and then maintain that wonderful characteristic – enthusiasm. I must repeat that I am not talking about an artificial or false enthusiasm (like on a gameshow), I am talking about real enthusiasm.

1. Do not be false or artificial – be genuine

Some people are blessed with natural enthusiasm that may have become automatic due to their conditioning – parental or environmental. Accept that whether you consider yourself naturally enthusiastic or not, anyone can easily develop this quality. So, as from this moment, it is within your grasp. It is not a question of whether you can, it is a question of whether you will.

Here are some sayings that might help and also act as reminders to you:

- To enjoy life you must touch much of it lightly.
- A candle loses none of its light by lighting another candle.
- It is not what happens – it is how you deal with it.
- Happiness is made to be shared.

■ Take care that the face which looks out from your mirror is a pleasant face. You may not see it again all day, but others will.

■ Cheerfulness is the atmosphere in which all things thrive.

■ It is not doing the things you like, but liking the things you have to do, that makes life happy.

■ Being alive is loving being alive.

■ A little smile adds a great deal to your face value.

■ You are never fully dressed without a smile.

So, take responsibility for generating your own enthusiasm.

2. Show your emotions – look and feel enthusiastic

Again, as with everything in life there is a balance to be struck. I am not suggesting in any way that we should all become extroverts. I said earlier that there is a link between passion and enthusiasm. So, become passionate; show passion in your conversation about your beliefs or your principles. Some people only show their passion – outside the work environment – about a hobby, sport, pastime or charity, when they suddenly come alive as individuals because of their passion. These people also command our respect.

Passion and enthusiasm are exhibited by voice change. We move our voice up or down and we speak faster. Our body language changes – the way that we move our arms, stand, lean forward, the way we walk or run, our facial expressions. These are all outward signs that others interpret as enthusiasm and passion, and we are in control of them. Try moving your voice up and down and speaking faster.

3. Formulate goals

Almost every chapter in a 'how to' section has goals as a prerequisite. How can you be enthusiastic about life without goals? How can you exhibit passion without enthusiasm or an objective or something you are aiming to succeed at? – for those goals stimulate happiness.

4. Practise physical techniques to promote your enthusiasm

Use your physiology to help build enthusiasm:

- Speak more rapidly.
- Change your voice inflection (intonation).
- Walk faster.
- Avoid slouching.
- Smile, don't frown (you use fewer muscles that way).
- Swing your arms while you walk – don't keep them in your pockets.
- Do not slur your speech.
- Breathe deeply.
- Be ready to laugh.
- Get excited about sharing with others.
- On the telephone, move your voice up and down.

5. Be cheerful

Try smiling now! Being miserable will cure absolutely nothing. It might get you some sympathy, but you and I both know that is no real help – in fact, it can make matters worse by making the situation last longer.

6. Show your enthusiasm to others

Be excited to meet, see and speak to people. Say to them, 'It's great to see you', I'm so glad you popped in', 'I'm thrilled you phoned', etc. Be enthusiastic on every occasion, whether it is a challenge, an opportunity, a fear or a drama. Approach everything with enthusiasm. You can, but will you?

THE POWER OF ENTHUSIASM

Enthusiasm is such a powerful force when harnessed. It enables us to overcome so many obstacles. It is irresistible. If you are an enthusiast right now, you know exactly what I am saying. If you have decided today to become an enthusiast, you will soon see success in whatever form, and, let me assure you, when enthusiasm is genuine and natural, happiness is much more likely to become a reality.

Pocket Reminders

- Be aware of the power of passion and enthusiasm
- Mix with enthusiastic people
- Note that enthusiasm is a state of mind and we have control over it.

Five tips on building your enthusiasm:

1. Do not be false or artificial – be genuine
2. Show emotion – look and feel enthusiastic
3. Formulate goals
4. Practise physical techniques to promote your enthusiasm
5. Be cheerful.

WISE WORDS

Years will wrinkle the skin, but lack of enthusiasm wrinkles the soul.

15

Self-motivation

Job advertisements demand it, employers hope for it, managers expect it, individuals claim to have it. But what is this elusive thing that everybody seems to want? It's self-motivation.

Do you have self-motivation, whatever it is? I believe we all have some form of self-motivation, even in its lowest form. For example, we require some sort of self-motivation in order to seek food.

Our pathway to success depends on how strong our levels of self-motivation are. The correlation between self-motivation and self-discipline was examined earlier, in Chapter 6 – Self-management. Is it self-motivation or self-discipline that makes me personally respond to the 6.30 am announcement from my bedside 'opportunity' clock?

PAIN AND PLEASURE

Anthony Robbins is perhaps one of the greatest teachers of personal development. His theories and principles about the practicalities of human behaviour revolve around two pillars: Pain and Pleasure.

Before we look at the negative aspects of pain, you must accept that pain has a positive element. For example, pain provides messages to the brain that prevent us harming our bodies. If we felt no pain, you could turn over logs in the fireplace and burn your hand in the process. So, pain provides continual feedback that prevents harm to our bodies.

The human brain will do almost anything to avoid pain (or its perception of pain) and to seek pleasure (or its perception of pleasure).

For example, let us take the simple practice of smoking. If it appears that there is more pain in giving up smoking, even though we know the harm that smoking does to the body and the risk of death or major illness, we still carry on. The immediate pain involved in giving up smoking may seem more painful than the long-term pain suffered by continuing smoking.

In order for you to give up smoking, a behavioural change has to happen. Now, you know within your heart that the reason you have purchased this book is to seek out a few ideas that will make you more successful and happy, and you must have known and accepted that some of these ideas will require change in some form. We can all change, that is not the problem – it is whether we are prepared to.

Behavioural change

The old country saying 'You can't teach an old dog new tricks' is, I am sure, true in the animal kingdom, but is completely wrong when we are dealing with the human brain. The problem is not 'can we?', but 'will we?'.

Ask yourself honestly, will you change?

Levels of motivation

The majority of us want to change, but have difficulty in taking the necessary action. The opportunity or attraction of perceived short-term pleasure outweighs in our mind the longer-term benefits. Below are a few tips that should help you to take the necessary steps to change, as well as improving your levels of self-motivation.

1. Visualize the result if you do not change

People generally think there is more pain in changing or taking action than there is in not doing so. So, to change, we must reverse this thought process. Think about, feel and visualize what will happen if you do not change. Make that result so fearful and see it so strongly and feel it so vividly that it is in turn more painful than the very tiny stages needed to change or reverse a habit or behaviour.

2. Visualize the result if you do change

Visualize the results after the change. Imagine what you will be like, how you will feel, how you will see yourself and others will see you. The rewards, experiences and activities that will come both during and at the end of this process are reason enough to change immediately.

3. Take a risk, do something different

As I mentioned earlier, you cannot expect different results if you continue doing the same thing over and over again.

In the most simple way, change is driven by self-motivation, and the self-motivation is stronger if we believe in the end result, if you believe that you can. The self-motivation again becomes stronger if you truly understand and accept the human behavioural attraction to pleasure and the avoidance of pain.

Let us look at two extremes, in graphic form, of how people go through their lives:

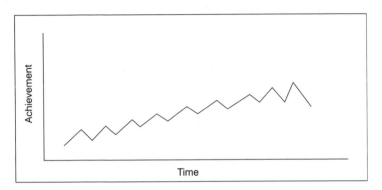

As you will see from the above graph, this person (a representative of the majority of people) has ups and downs, but they are fairly small. This graph of life exhibits fairly low self-motivation. It also exhibits an unwillingness to take risks, as well as powerful fear of perceived pain.

Now let us look at our high-achiever's graph.

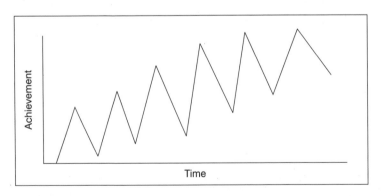

This, as you see, has enormous leaps as well as vast plunges into the depths, but exhibits a preparedness for risk. There are highs and lows of what could be called success and failure, and almost certainly it is the graph of a winner, an achiever and of a person leaving his or her mark on the world. However, I am not necessarily saying that this is a graph of happiness.

The second graph demonstrates self-motivation and a willingness to take decisions and actions. It shows that during a failure or downturn, the principles – faith and psychology – of how to bounce back again into the next leap forward are still available. This flow also exhibits a positive self-image and a propensity for turning setbacks into opportunities.

4. Have a good look at yourself

How do you see yourself? You may look in the mirror if you like, but that is not particularly necessary. Are you dissatisfied, or are you content? Are you ambitious? Are you enthusiastic, nervous or shy? Do you consider yourself good company? Do you think you are overweight or too skinny?

It is fascinating how people see themselves. We are all no doubt familiar with the effects of some of the tragic mental illnesses, such as anorexia nervosa, in which a basically slim individual sees themself as overweight and goes to unbelievable lengths in attempting to keep food out of their body. The reverse example is of how very overweight people do not see themselves as being overweight, perhaps because in their minds they only compare themselves with people who are much, much heavier than they are.

5. Change your image

Your self-image will change according to your goals, purpose, faith and beliefs, as well as the events of your life and your success experiences. Self-image will change according to the environmental conditioning that you experience, and self-image automatically changes through conscious or subconscious behaviour.

Have you noticed how some people walk differently when they come out of the hairdresser's? Or how some people will behave differently in different clothes? You put men or women into special-occasion clothes – evening dress or dinner jacket – and they will walk and behave differently. Their self-image has changed. When people lose weight or give up an acknowledged bad habit, there is a change in their self-image – usually for the better. They seem to have greater pride, greater self-respect, and display a positive outlook.

BECOMING MORE MOTIVATED

There are a number of stages we can follow in order to become even more self-motivated. These same stages can be taught to others by those of you who are parents or leaders.

1. Set motivation goals

Self-motivation has at its heart goals and purpose.

2. Mix with motivated people

Mix with motivated people, as demotivated people can and will demoralize you. In Chapter 14 – Irresistible Enthusiasm, we discussed the contagious effect of enthusiasm. Motivation can also be contagious, particularly if we are in the right environment.

The more we mix with people who exhibit the positive characteristics which we seek, the more quickly we will adopt them ourselves. Likewise, it is just as important to avoid the opposite.

3. Keep making positive affirmations

Why say, 'I can't', or 'I'm scared'? It is just as easy to say the opposite. Is it just that we do not want to appear too arrogant or too clever? Sometimes, in order to be accepted or liked, we are too modest. But we know deep down that the more we make positive affirmations, the more likely we are to bring about a positive result.

4. Make a commitment to be motivated

Decide that you are going to be a motivated person and that others will recognize you as owning that elusive characteristic – self-motivation. Today and every day, make that commitment – all it takes is the decision.

5. Monitor your progress

Seeing yourself progress is motivational. Most people set some goals at the begining of the year – New Year resolutions. It is at this time that one looks back over the previous 12 months. If they were not successful – if, for example, a person has borrowed more money, is deeper in debt, their career has stood still, and tangible acquisitions or achievements in life have not been forthcoming – it is understandable that that person will feel less motivated. However, if, on the other hand, the previous 12 months have been successful – for example, savings have increased, less is owed to the mortgage company or there has been career progression – it is just as understandable that that individual will be more motivated.

This principle is one of the laws of motivation and is a key factor for managers in motivating others. A good manager will endeavour in every way to ensure that his or her team is progressing. So if you and I wish to develop our own self-motivation, it is very important to explore all the areas in our life where we are progressing and concentrate our thoughts on those areas. We could take a very simple sporting analogy, as told to me by many friends who play golf. If they have a good round, they go back to the clubhouse and are raring to get going next time. On the other hand, if they have a bad round, when they get back to the clubhouse they are less enthusiastic and perhaps even question why they took up the silly game in the first place.

6. Set realistic challenges

Life is full of opportunities. Some of these are challenges, but if you accept a challenge in whatever form while believing deep down that you cannot win, you will not be motivated.

I have seen this principle causing turmoil in so many organizations, perhaps most significantly in salesmanship, where a manager sets a target or an incentive competition and the majority of the salespeople know they have no chance of meeting that target or participating in the reward.

When this happens, not only is motivation lost, it is replaced with demotivation. If you recall, in Chapter 7 – Goals: The Purpose of Life, I stressed the importance of having immediate goals that you know you can achieve. You can also have longer-term goals that you hope you will achieve, having given yourself time. So, once again, be realistic – challenge only motivates if it is possible for you to win.

7. Change your routine

There are many activities that can change our attitude, thoughts and behaviour and will get us looking forward to the next day. These activities really build self-motivation. Throughout their lives, most people have a behavioural pattern that is built around routine. Although routine is essential to build confidence and create security, it is not necessarily conducive to enhancing self-motivation. Small things like moving the furniture in your home, changing your office layout, or taking a different route to work, are all part of breaking a pattern, which in turn can be stimulating.

8. Motivate someone else

Give yourself the challenge of motivating another person every day. One of the principles of success that recurs throughout this book is the idea that what you hand out in life, you get back. I speak at conferences and seminars in many countries and there are certain times of the year when my workload is intense. I have been asked on many occasions if I get tired or exhausted, and I can honestly say that there are times when I do need a bit of a break. But my brain is motivated and inspired when I hear and see other people's success stories, when I have imparted my messages at one event and I meet people from that audience again in the future and they share their stories. It is extremely hard to describe the motivation and the recharge to one's own batteries from other people's success experiences. If you set out to motivate one person every day of your life, you cannot help but become a completely self-motivated individual.

9. Invest in learning materials

Self-motivation is stimulated by new ideas. Make it a managed habit to continually acquire books and CDs and build a personal development library, using your vehicle as a learning centre as well as a means of transport. When we are stimulated by new ideas, we become more motivated.

10. Keep fit and healthy

When I first started on the speaking circuit, I found it essential to ensure that the adrenalin was running, and a few minutes prior to making my presentation, I would try to get into a room on my own and do 20 or 30 quick press-ups. I have found throughout my life that the more fit the body is, the more able is the brain. As life expectancy in the Western world increases every decade, there is even more reason to take responsibility for your body and keep it fit and healthy. The quality of life in those wonderful 'twilight' years will be dramatically enhanced if you have a fit and healthy body. In most cases it is your decision.

You will very rarely meet self-motivated people who have not taken physical responsibility for their bodies, keeping them fit and well through healthy eating and exercise.

11. Set realistic challenges

Self-motivation will fluctuate. Managers recognize that motivation, once established within a group of people, does not last. Maintaining it is a continuous process, and so it must be with you and me in managing ourselves.

As we saw in the earlier graph, life is full of ups and downs, so there are days when you will feel less motivated, and those are the days when by reading through some of these key points and putting them back into action, you will re-establish your own self-motivation.

Very few people have another person whose sole task is to motivate them.

12. Do not become a self-development junkie

This is a self-motivation warning. With the plethora of books, videos, CDs, articles and numerous courses on personal development which are now available, I am very sad to say that over the last few years I have met an increasing number of what I can only describe as personal development or motivational junkies. I meet them at seminars, conferences and events. They are full of talk and full of promises. They want to stand up and speak, they have read all the books, they know all the jargon, but they do absolutely nothing with this knowledge in their lives. Every day is devoted to the next book, the next course or the next seminar. The ideas distilled in this book are here to be used.

Pocket Reminders

- Our pathway to success depends on our levels of self-motivation

- Understand the two principles of pleasure and pain (the latter is not always negative)

- To be successful we often need to make changes.

Five tips on helping you take the necessary steps to change:

1. Visualize the result if you *do not* change

2. Visualize the result if you *do* change

3. Take a risk, do something different

4. Have a good look at yourself

5. Change your image.

Twelve stages to self-motivation:

1. Set motivation goals

2. Mix with motivated people

3. Keep making positive affirmations

4. Make a commitment to be motivated

5. Monitor your progression

6. Set realistic challenges

7. Change your routine

8. Motivate someone else

9. Invest in learning materials

10. Keep fit and healthy

11. Motivation is a continuous process

12. Do not become a self-development junkie.

WISE WORDS

When you can think of yesterday without regret and of tomorrow without fear, then you are on the road to success.

16

Communication

There are a multitude of ways in which we communicate:

- body language;
- speech;
- writing;
- radio;
- telephone;
- television;
- facsimile;
- e-mail;
- the internet.

HOW WE COMMUNICATE

Less than 10 per cent of all communication skills are verbal. There is obviously therefore more to communication than just being able to talk.

The five major senses that we use to process information are:

- sight (visual);
- touch (kinaesthetic);
- hearing (auditory);
- taste (gustatory);
- smell (olfactory).

The three major communication areas are, of course, seeing, feeling and hearing, and we all use all three if we are fortunate. Of course, we are all different and we will each use one area more than the other two. For example, a person who processes information by the way they look at something is more of a 'seeing person' (visual), whereas another who prefers to process information by the way they feel is more of a 'feeling person' (kinaesthetic), and another who mainly processes information by the way it sounds is a 'hearing person' (auditory).

So, to begin with, how do you process information? Suppose you are buying a car. Which would be the most important?

- the style, colour, shape or make;
- whether it 'feels right' and is comfortable; or
- the sound of the engine or the number of squeaks and rattles.

Now, of course you may well use all three senses, but one predominantly. If the look of the car is of prime importance, then you will be predominantly visual. If the feeling is of prime importance, you will be predominantly kinaesthetic. If the sound of the car is of prime importance, then you will be predominantly auditory.

Now look at some examples of various phrases. First, a visual person:

- 'I see the sense...'
- 'It appears to me...'

- 'It looks to me like...'
- 'We see eye to eye...'

This person will more than likely greet you with a phrase like 'Nice to *see* you.'

Kinaesthetic key phrases are:

- 'It feels right...'
- 'Let's get to grips with...'
- 'Hand in hand...'
- 'It slipped my mind...'
- 'Let's lay cards on the table...'

This person, more than likely, would greet you by saying, '*How* are you?'

Finally, the auditory key phrases:

- 'I hear what you are saying...'
- 'It rings a bell...'
- 'Loud and clear...'
- 'Unheard of...'
- 'Word for word...'

This kind of person will more than likely greet you with 'I *heard* you were coming today' or 'I *hear* things are going well for you.'

So, these three major senses are very important. In order to ensure good communication, first understand your predominant form of communication, and secondly, be able to recognize other people's. One often hears about 'chemistry', but this is, of course, communication rapport. Have you ever met somebody for the first time and instinctively disliked them or they you? Well, of course there could be numerous reasons, but perhaps the chemistry was not right.

Now, you are not in control of their communication, but you are most certainly in control of your own.

The importance of listening

Perhaps the most important guideline here is to be able to listen actively and, if you wish, echo the phrases used by the other person. I am not saying you have got to copy them word for word and I am most certainly not saying you have to change and behave in an artificial manner – but I am saying it is up to you, in achieving success and happiness, to become an effective communicator. I mean really listen, concentrate, and watch the other person's lips. Possibly the greatest attribute for people who are trusted and respected by others is their willingness and ability to listen. Don't use your imagination in trying to read between the lines or imagine what the other person is saying before they have said it. You will end up misunderstanding, which will have a negative result.

Communication is a tool for you to master and use in your ascent towards success. I am certainly not going to claim that this is a characteristic of all so-called successful people, but I bet you agree that the ability to communicate effectively and a pleasing personality are characteristics of all happy people. So, that must be a good enough reason to make this one of the steps to success and getting what you want through life.

A good communicator attracts other people. If you succeed as a communicator, people will want to be with you, share with you, seek your counsel, trust you and invite you. The art of communication, in so many cases, is the ability to convey information or a message from one person to another with absolute clarity.

IMPROVING COMMUNICATION

We can now discuss some ideas that will help us towards better communication:

1. It's good to talk

Major conflicts in the world are not solved in the killing-fields. It is when politicians communicate and can keep talking that there has to be hope. We can take that same principle into business, into our personal lives and our relationships. As long as we keep talking, conflict can be avoided.

2. Respect the people you talk to

Communication is about relationships, and you will be a better communicator, verbally and non-verbally, if you respect the other person. The phrase 'See the oak tree, not the acorn' is a worthwhile reminder.

When you treat people like 'acorns', they will react sometimes with hurt, sometimes with annoyance, sometimes with aggression. But if you treat everybody not necessarily for what they are but what they might become, you can create a more conducive situation for communication that, in turn, will achieve the desired result.

Be honest with yourself, have you ever formed an opinion of someone from his or her appearance and then discovered you were completely wrong? If you treat everybody as an 'oak tree', you cannot help but be a good communicator.

3. Give compliments

Try always to have something nice to say. Look for every opportunity to give a compliment. Seek out the occasions when a little praise can be passed on.

I was very fortunate to work with Sir David Frost, the TV personality, for a couple of years. One of the most admirable qualities that he exhibited, apart from being a very positive personality, was that he always had something pleasant to say to whoever he met. He genuinely meant the compliment, and found it easy to give praise. I might also add that his other particularly admirable characteristic was the total trust he inspired in every world leader he met and famous people throughout every walk of life. He never betrayed a confidence, never gossiped and never said one nasty or unpleasant thing about any other person. That truly is not only extremely difficult, but also a most admirable human trait, and in turn is perhaps why he has become such a successful broadcaster and why he can interview the most powerful people in the world.

4. Speak less than you listen

We have all been given two ears and one mouth, and that is the ratio in which they are most effectively used in conversation. We learn more by listening than by talking, and this is the hallmark of a great conversationalist.

So, in conversation, concentrate on what the other person is saying. Look into their eyes and their face, read their body language, and give them total and complete attention. Many people do not really listen when they are not talking – they are actually thinking what they are going to say next.

I teach salespeople the importance of asking questions and gathering information. A good conversationalist is the person who will ask and probe and get the other person talking.

5. Be interested in others

Many of us are told the importance of having to sell oneself, and if this is related to the skills of selling, one would naturally assume that in order to sell oneself one had to talk about oneself. In reality, the opposite is true. To do this effectively, one should be interested in the other person: find out their interests, worries or experiences. To be interesting, all you have to do is to be interested.

6. Make sure your criticism is constructive

From time to time it may be necessary in all relationships, whether at work or at home, to constructively criticize another. If this situation arises, as a good communicator you will criticize the performance, not the performer. Let me emphasize again, success is achieved with and through people. Creating enemies is not conducive to longer-lasting happiness and success.

So, on the occasions when it is necessary to correct, guide or improve another person's performance or behaviour, do not criticize the individual, criticize the result. Try not to use the word 'you', and make it very clear that what you are trying to do is correct the event. Look at what went wrong, and the result of what that person has done, and ask or discuss what, next time, they would do differently.

7. Make sure you understand what is said before replying

So much of communication breakdown is due to misunderstanding. It is not what you say that is important, it is what the other person hears. This equally applies to yourself.

Listen to what is said to you, and if you are in any doubt at all, repeat what you hear with a question in order to confirm. Try saying, for example, 'Am I right in understanding that you said...?' If you are in the situation of giving instructions, ask the other person to repeat the instruction.

8. Share

Good communication is really all about building relationships, so one has to be a bit of a psychologist. This is important, as we are all dealing with people and trying to understand their feelings. Do share your 'give up' goals (ie becoming fitter, losing weight, stopping smoking, etc) with family, colleagues and even acquaintances, but be very careful with whom you share your 'success' goals.

WRITTEN COMMUNICATION

The golden rule of written communication is always to write positively. It is only ever in the last and final resort that you should use the written word to be critical in any form at all.

On the occasions when you are put into the position of having to write critically to someone, at least the other person has the opportunity of either justifying, explaining or at least imparting his or her thoughts and reasons.

But the danger with the written word is nearly always that more is read into what is written than perhaps was in the mind of the writer. The written word can be misinterpreted. The written word can be repeatedly re-read.

So, on your pathway to success, try to make it a golden rule never to resort to the written word when being critical. In business, the inter-office memo causes more strife and misery than any other form of communication. It is not a method of management, but sometimes it is used in this way with disastrous results.

It should be avoided in family situations, too. I personally know that when I have written to my sons in a critical way, they have said to me afterwards that they would have much preferred me to have spoken to them rather than writing.

E-mail is becoming probably the world's biggest timewaster – a most brilliant tool of communication being abused. In my book *Communicate to Win*, I discuss the most effective use of this incredible technology in more detail. So instead of sending an e-mail internally, walk across the office, talk to someone face to face. It saves time in most cases, and it helps to build relationships. Do try to send less e-mail and to talk more.

Care about others

Make it a habit to send nice notes, cards, e-mails, letters and thank-yous. It is more and more appreciated these days (when our postboxes are full of direct mail) to receive a personal letter or note from a friend or colleague. It is so much nicer to receive a written invitation than a phone call, or a note of thanks rather than a verbal thank-you. Success is achieved so much more easily with the support and encouragement of other people. It's what you do with who you know that will certainly make you a lucky person. It is quite extraordinarily true that if you care about other people, they will care about you.

BODY LANGUAGE

Now let us briefly discuss body language. There are many books available where this subject is discussed and illustrated in detail. So, the purpose here is just to bring it to your attention, since I began this chapter by saying that it is a prime area of communication.

In any conversation, as well as speaking and listening, we watch facial expressions and other body signals. There are approximately 40,000 words and sounds available to us all.

We use approximately 4,000 on a daily basis. In the imprecise science of body language, it is claimed there are some 750,000 body language signals, of which 15,000 are from the face alone. Those two statistics show that the majority of people can control what they say. But with 750,000 body language signals, it is impossible to control what we are giving away.

So, when the spoken word is in conflict with the body language signal, the body language will give you the correct information. Therefore if, on being introduced to you, somebody says, 'I am so pleased to meet you', but his or her body language gives you a completely different signal, the body language conveys the true thoughts in that person's mind.

So, as a successful communicator, first build your own understanding of body language – watch people. Read a book or two on this fascinating subject and you will soon build your own understanding and interpretation.

CONSIDER THE FEELINGS OF OTHERS

Do remain aware that we will all be affected by environments, people and their feelings. When people are depressed, they tend to depress those around them. One elderly friend of mine, a grand lady in her seventy-ninth year, reminds her old friends and neighbours when they pop in to see her to leave their aches, pains and moans at the door. Surprisingly, they do just that.

I hope that I have demonstrated that success is achieved either with or through people, so this vast subject of communication in all its various forms is integral to how you and I relate to our connections.

Communication is desperately important. Throughout the world, it seems that when people stop talking, they fight. It also seems that even in the more advanced Western societies, some people of poorer or limited education, with perhaps little command of their language, resort, through frustration, to fighting as they are unable to communicate through the spoken word.

Finally, remember, it takes two to quarrel, but only one to end it.

Pocket Reminders

■ Less than 10 per cent of all communication skills are verbal.

Eight tips to improve our verbal communication:

1. Remember, it's good to talk
2. Respect the people you talk to
3. Give compliments
4. Speak less than you listen
5. Be interested in others
6. Make only constructive criticism
7. Make sure you understand what is said before replying
8. Share.

Tips to improve our written communication:

■ Take care – always write positively
■ Write to thank others.

WISE WORDS

Great minds have purpose, others have wishes.

17

Success at Home

In my opinion, one of the tragedies of the modern world, certainly in the United Kingdom, has been the break-up of the family unit. Whether one looks back to the early part of the 20th century as the good old days or the bad old days, nevertheless, tremendous strength and goodness could be drawn from the traditional family unit.

Many things have been blamed on the break-up of the family unit: increased crime statistics, loneliness, doctors' surgeries filled with patients who are not really clinically ill but are there through worry and stress.

Now this may all sound rather depressing, but it need not be. I believe the great value of the past is as a lesson so that we can make tomorrow a better day. One can obtain great strength and joy through having a partner and being part of a family, as long as there is regular contact, sharing and caring, and an absence of jealousy.

THE BENEFITS OF A FAMILY

If you are fortunate enough to have a partner or family, do they thrill to the sound of your footsteps when you come in? What a goal that could be for every one of us. I consider having a strong family to be one of the main purposes of life. I have been fortunate enough to experience the enormous joy, security, love, warmth and affection that come from being part of a family.

My parents had four sons and they set a great example in not only keeping us closely together, but making sure that, as we got married and grandchildren came along, our family remained strongly united.

I believe that everybody should have a purpose in life. Some people believe their purpose is purely monetary: to amass as much money or power as possible. For others it may be to achieve recognition, to be promoted, or to be acclaimed. However, in the process of their single-minded striving towards these goals, they may leave a trail of destruction behind them. On the way they may well have married and had children, but the day will come when they suddenly look back at the years gone by and realize what they have really missed. They may well be the Chairman of the Board or have millions invested, or be a sporting superstar, but they are lonely and unhappy, continually saying, 'If only!' If every parent looked after his or her own children, many of the world's problems would be solved.

Some years ago, we had neighbours who were very much the 'do-gooder' type. They went to church three times on a Sunday and were very involved in church youth groups – so much so, that they dedicated all their spare time in this direction.

They had three children. Their eldest son became more and more uncontrollable as he got into his late teens. At that time, I had a Lancia Spider sports car (a little hobby of mine). Well, we went away on holiday and, on returning, found that the garage was empty and my Spider was gone. It was eventually found 5 miles away with the sump knocked off and the engine seized. It turned out that the car had been stolen and dumped by my next door neighbour's son.

I was obviously concerned and did not want the police to take action, so I went to see the boy's father, with whom I was on good terms, and said, 'I have bad news and I am terribly embarrassed and sorry to say that Peter was the one who took my car', and I showed him the evidence. His reply was 'I am so sorry and upset; I will phone my wife and she will go straight to church and say a prayer.'

Well, the sad story is that that young lad ended up repeatedly in and out of jail for offence after offence. This is not a criticism of attending a place of worship, but more a criticism of that family's way of practising the teachings of their place of worship. We have all heard the expression 'Charity begins at home.' Look after your own first, and then you will be in a position to help look after others.

Relatives

Now some of my readers may not have their own family. This does not mean to say that they cannot be successful or happy. All I wish to emphasize is that if you do have a family, even if it is only distant relatives, value them and keep in contact. During our lives, most of us will have lots of friends and many acquaintances. We all know that our true friends can be counted on the fingers of one hand,

and that is why I emphasize again that you must value your family.

Marriage

In the past, people got married at a very young age. More recently, partners have tended to be older, so many marriages start with high expectations. People expect their partners to make them happy because they looked forward to being with them prior to marriage, and yet divorce statistics have reached a horrifying level.

Successful marriages are not based upon what any one party expects or can *take out* of the relationship – they are built upon what one *puts into* them. Love can be very fickle – it is something that takes time to truly build. So, to build a relationship through marriage requires effort, but the so-called price is well worth paying.

One has to earn loyalty, respect and love, and one can only earn these by being prepared to contribute and compromise. This brings us back to the law of success that says that whatever you hand out in life, you get back.

Let us run through a few ideas that help to build and maintain enjoyment, happiness and security through family success.

1. Eat together regularly

I have noticed a trend that I find horrifying – people living together in the same house rarely, if ever, eat together. The parent(s) buy the food and may even cook it, but it seems meals are eaten at different times and/or even eaten in front of the television. I have met young people aged between 19 and 22 who have never sat at a table in a private house and eaten a complete meal.

This has to be one of the most important activities of any family: to lay a table and for all to sit and eat together. If it is completely impossible due to working hours, then it can be done at weekends. There must be no excuse whatsoever for neglecting this important family activity. Mealtimes can be a valuable opportunity to see each other, relax and converse. By contrast, sitting in front of a television with a plate of food balanced on one's knees will elicit a grunt at best!

2. Share opinions

I suggest that you regularly ask your family members for their opinions.

It can be so trying when there is one rather opinionated member of a family who holds forth and does not give others a chance to voice their opinion.

By asking other people their opinion, we can learn so much. It develops communication, and whether you agree with the opinion of others or not is of no matter. Some of those opinions may well be valuable and worthwhile.

I have personally found that over the years, the opinions of my own children have been stimulating, and in many cases full of wisdom. I have benefited enormously from their thoughts and ideas. So, if you are going to ask others for their opinions, remember to listen to them.

3. Maximize the opportunities for happiness

Families are of course all about relationships, and, as we all know, relationships can occasionally go wrong – one can fall in love, but also out of love. To maximize the opportunities for happiness within the family, try to concentrate on the good points. Do not dwell on that bad or annoying habit. Whenever people live together, they cannot help but become irritated from time to time. It is normal and under-standable, but that does not mean to say that it is all one should see. Get over that irritation, concentrate on the whole and replace the negative feelings in your mind with positive ones.

4. Be there when you are needed

Whenever you are needed by a member of your family, be there. Value those special occasions and make every effort never to miss an important family event. The only things we ever regret in life are the things we did not do – not the things we did.

Perhaps one of my greatest regrets relates to an occasion when I was returning from a business trip to the Arabian Gulf after four months. When I arrived back at Heathrow Airport, I found my partners had let me down. They had promised a car and money on my arrival, but neither of these materialized. I had arranged to fly to Scotland to play in the fathers' cricket match with my second son, Walter, who was in the first XI cricket team. I had played in the match a year previously, when my eldest son, Lyster, had qualified for the team.

I eventually managed to get on the plane to Scotland with my wife and we managed to get some transport to the school, but I now had no English currency and it took me about an hour to get hold of some money.

Well, I arrived too late for the match and another parent played in my place. I cannot describe the sadness and despair that I experienced sitting on the boundary watching Walter run in to bowl not being able to be part of that occasion.

So, with hindsight, I should have considered my priorities, played in the match and forgone the money. Create a culture within your immediate family such that whenever you are needed for an occasion, advice, counsel or support, it takes precedence over everything else.

5. Show emotion

In Victorian times, it was not the done thing to show affection or emotion. It was the era of the stiff upper lip, when the best antidote to most emotions was a cold bath.

> When my sons were in their mid-teens, my wife remarked one day, 'I don't know why you don't kiss them.' My reaction was 'Well, they're boys and I'm a man, you don't do things like that.' But then it occurred to me: why ever not? So, if you want to create a culture of family success, cuddle, kiss, touch and hold your family – you will be amazed by the results. Your family will feel more secure, more cared for and more loved. Yes, I know it is common sense, but often we are so busy that we do not have the time for a cuddle, or perhaps we feel silly holding hands or kissing.

6. Saying 'I love you'

Three of the most powerful words that any person can say to another are 'I love you', but these words are so under-utilized later in life, once the heady days of courtship are over. Just think how many fences can be mended with those words. Many people have great difficulty in saying them, while others just forget, or it just does not occur to them how important it is to restate those powerful words.

7. Plan to play

Remember the powerful adage 'A family that plays together, stays together.' It only takes one member of the family to suggest, plan and then create opportunities to play. Differences can be forgotten and wounds can be healed when people play together. There are stories to tell and experiences to share. It is all too easy to use the excuses of time or pressure not to play. For some mature people, it is necessary for them to learn to play again, to leave their egos at the front door and play on the floor with youngsters. Learn to be a child again – behaving like a child occasionally can give you a whole new perspective on your values and assumptions.

8. Encourage humour – laugh at yourself

Humour is such a leveller, so learn to laugh again. Almost every crisis can be solved with humour, and laughter is one of the greatest joys of being human and one of the fundamental differences between humans and the animal world. There are some people who are brilliant at telling jokes or stories and there are others of us who are not, but one does not need to be a comedian to be able to laugh at a humorous situation. How about being able to laugh at yourself? It is frustrating to be with people who take themselves too seriously.

We all look silly from time to time, but so what? If you can laugh at yourself occasionally, you will encourage others to laugh with you. It means someone else is happy, so take pleasure out of their enjoyment. As always, there is a balance to be struck: it can be extremely annoying when you stub your toe on the foot of the bed and your partner rolls out of bed holding their sides, laughing at your misfortune!

9. Remember the purpose of life

Those of my readers who are striving in their careers and are under pressure to achieve may be putting in long hours and may even have to travel away from home. Remember the purpose of life. If you are a parent and you have a family, remember the purpose of all your endeavour – it is not to be the richest man in the graveyard; it is not to be the great provider that your family despise and treat as a stranger. So plan on spending quality time with those you love and care for. This quality time (whether it be in playing, talking, listening, or just being together) should take priority over any possible interruption. Let your family know that this time is absolutely precious and that even though you may be striving for monetary success, promotion or achievement, the purpose of all this endeavour is to benefit your family, not to achieve some remote future goal.

So, live life in the present, enjoy each moment, value each event: be able to stop and admire a flower that bursts into bloom, or the baby who stands for the first time, or the child who returns home from school with some success, or the partner who has something to share.

10. Compliment your family

Ask yourself whether you really look for the opportunity to give compliments. What are your expectations of the members of your family? As a parent, do you expect too much from your children? Are you putting them under pressure to achieve, so that you can gain the satisfaction or the pride?

I was fortunate that both my parents expected little from their four sons, and the consequence was that none of us was put under pressure to perform, to be a high achiever, or to make up for any inadequacies our parents may have had;

and whenever any of us did achieve, there was genuine excitement and enthusiasm and immense pride.

Anyone can give a compliment – reverse the tendency to look for an opportunity to criticize or find fault and seek out the opportunities for complimenting your family. Be aware of the sadness and stress that some parents and their offspring go through when expectations are too high.

11. Create surprises

Whether you are a parent or a member of the family, from time to time create occasions when you can give the others a surprise. As we mature in life, our greatest pleasures and joys do not come from receiving, but from giving. It is wonderful to be on the receiving end of a surprise, and it is equally good fun to plan surprises. These exercises somehow bond families more strongly together. Surprises take just a little bit of time, planning and effort, but give wonderful results.

12. Keep in touch

The moving apart of families, because of the opportunities and demands of our modern lifestyles, is a trend that is unlikely to be reversed. If this happens in your family, and some of your family live far away, there is no excuse for losing touch. What about birthdays and anniversaries? What does it really cost to send a card? In monetary terms, virtually nothing; in time and effort, a little, but to show that you care is well worth that tiny sacrifice.

13. Forgive

From time to time, in every family there will be an upset. Somebody will do or say something hurtful, and if you are on the receiving end, it is normal to react angrily. You might even say something like 'I'll never forgive you' – what a negative message to plant in your brain. Whenever we say that, we relive, remind ourselves and re-visualize the event of that hurt.

Can we change the event? Of course not – it is now history, so try never to say, 'I'll never forgive.' It will not make you happy to bear that grudge, nor will it prevent that occurrence happening again. It will do no good whatsoever and will fester and cause you, the thinker, distress. So get over the hurt. Often, the easiest and quickest way is to ask yourself, 'Why did he say that?', 'Why did she do that?' Even if you don't come up with a logical answer, at least you've tried to approach the situation with some understanding.

It is absolutely essential in every family to be able to forgive and forget and concentrate on the future. You may even have learnt a little lesson that in the future will be of benefit to all.

14. Build your own life and interests

For those of my readers who might classify themselves as 'home executives', dedicated to the care of the home and the rearing of children (which is, of course, a career in itself), remember that at some stage children will depart; they will want to lead their own lives and follow their own interests. It is therefore essential that while you may be dedicating a large part of your activities, interests and endeavours in their direction, you remember to also build a life for yourself.

I have come across too many parents who experience a dreadful vacuum and loneliness when their children leave home. They cannot understand why the devotion they have shown to their children appears not to be reciprocated. So always, whoever you are and whatever you do, have some interests, a hobby, or part-time employment.

15. Have something to look forward to

This is different from creating a surprise. Every family should have something that they are jointly looking forward to. The most obvious is a family holiday, but in between holidays there are lots of other ideas that one can create. Again, all this takes is a little bit of thought and planning.

16. Have some family rules

You know the expression 'If one does not stand for something, one will fall for anything.' The leaders of any family should provide the strength behind and set the standards of that family's philosophy and culture. As (one of) the leaders, be conscious that if you set the example, you will not need to use the rule book. Through my own experience, I have found four very strong principles, or rules, that in my opinion should under no circumstances be broken within a family.

- First, as a parent, understand that all children and young people will make mistakes and perhaps even drive you to distraction, but ensure they are aware of the barrier beyond which they must never go. We all know that a well-trained pet is a happy pet, and exactly the same principle applies with children. Give them happiness and strength and security by knowing the limits beyond which they must not go.
- Secondly, make it a family rule to always be truthful and honest and never to lie. Never punish the truth, but by all means punish a lie.
- Thirdly, bad manners towards other family members and those outside the family should not be tolerated. Rudeness is an offence to the family and is therefore unacceptable.
- Fourthly, create security through self-discipline. There should be a balance here; it should be a caring, sharing discipline, where everybody knows where they stand. For example, it can comprise the sharing of duties such as washing up, tidying up, laying the table and cleaning the bathroom, and

these duties should be shared between all, and I mean all, members of the family. Create this self-discipline and it will in turn create strength, which will be so powerful in the face of temptations later on in life.

17. Share the joys and worries

Lastly, share those joys and worries. If you cannot share your worries with your immediate family, you will most certainly be a very sad and lonely person. Some people experience great monetary loss or pressure, often at times of recession, in many cases through no fault of their own. That financial burden can be so great, some end up taking their own life because they have kept the burden to themselves. It's only money – what a ridiculous thing to give up one's life for.

There is wonderful strength in a close family. So share those worries, not to make your family suffer, but to give them a chance to understand. The sharing will almost certainly strengthen and unite the family, which will become a platform for outstanding success in the future.

Pocket Reminders

- Eat together regularly
- Share opinions
- Maximize the opportunity for happiness
- Be there when you are needed
- Show emotion
- Say 'I love you'
- Plan to play
- Encourage humour – laugh at yourself

- Remember the purpose of life
- Compliment your family
- Create surprises
- Keep in touch
- Forgive
- Build your own life and interests
- Have something to look forward to
- Have some family rules
- Share your joys and worries.

WISE WORDS

Never get so busy making a living that you forget to make a life.

A good marriage is a prize... you do not get it for nothing.

Children have more need of models... than critics.

18

Financial Success

One of the major goals of many people is to amass a great deal of money, and in this chapter I will give you my views on this important aspect of success.

In the Introduction, I stated that success without happiness is not really success and I gave the example of Nicholas Darvas, who, although fabulously rich, complained that he was unhappy because others were richer than he, and got no enjoyment out of his success and wealth. I do not think that to have wealth is wrong at all and I believe that to have the goal of becoming wealthy is perfectly reasonable.

MONEY VS HAPPINESS

I feel I should warn you that amassing money for its own sake will not guarantee happiness, although many will classify you as successful. Even so, I am a real enthusiast about making money. This book can be used to make you money if that is your goal. Remember that the purpose of making money is to be able to spend it on your goals – the pleasure comes when you use the money on those goals.

One Christmas Eve, I was with my accountant, Robert Raynes, and, having concluded our meeting over my affairs, we started to philosophize. He asked me a most profound question: 'Why is it, Richard, that some of my most wealthy clients are some of the most miserable and difficult to work with?'

As you can imagine, we both had our opinions. But I felt that the question was really rather sad. Why is it that those who just strive after money do not make themselves happy? We all know the misquoted and misunderstood cliché 'Money is the root of all evil.' The real quotation, from the Bible, is 'Love of money is the root of all evil.' This is very different. The love of money for itself may be the cause of the unhappiness that amassing wealth can bring. In having the legitimate goal of becoming wealthy, I believe that you need to keep in mind what I call the 'balance of life'.

In the modern world today, there are almost limitless opportunities for making your fortune. In order to make a lot of money, I believe you must have a very good understanding of what it is and must also be aware of the harm it can cause as well as the enjoyment and the rewards that it can provide.

Money is a commodity that has value only when it is exchanged for something else, like property or services rendered, for example. Money only provides us with pleasure, enjoyment, prosperity and happiness when we get rid of it by trading with others for their services and their products.

In Britain, we often use the expressions 'new money' and 'old money'. Old money, in most cases, is understood to be that held by the aristocracy and those who have inherited money from their ancestors. The way old money is handled is very different from the way new money is handled. First, those with old money often find it distasteful to talk about it, perhaps because they did not make it, or perhaps because, equally interestingly, they are in many cases better able to keep its importance in proportion. Of course, one can always think of exceptions to the rule.

Many of those making new money have, and are driven by, all manner of goals and ambitions as well as fears. Many wish to provide better education and a better lifestyle for their children than they themselves have experienced.

Some people have a burning ambition to leave a fortune for their children. I have to confess that this is perhaps one of the least of my priorities. When my sons were in their teens, we had many family discussions and I explained that I had no desire to work all my life and leave them with an inheritance that I could have spent and enjoyed. It does not inspire me to be the wealthiest man in the graveyard, nor do I wish to give others satisfaction when they look at the published wills column in a newspaper to see how much I or my wife may have left.

So why is it that the wealthiest clients of my accountant are some of the most miserable? First, you have to accept that amassing money is not a basis for happiness; secondly, it is of limited value just sitting in the bank; thirdly, it is human nature for people to become fearful of being without their money and worried that they might lose it. People fight harder for anything they fear they might lose or have taken away from them, and so they strive even harder to acquire those things.

HOW MUCH MONEY DO YOU NEED?

One of the hardest questions that you need to ask yourself is how much money you need or want. Those, of course, are two completely different questions. I have wrestled with these over the years and they are very difficult to answer. How much do we really need? You can look at your current lifestyle and compare it with the lifestyle you wish to have.

As the years go by, though, you will need to take into account inflation and changing circumstances. How much will you need then?

One of my dearest friends, CJ, retired to the island of Ibiza with his wife at the age of 42. He had discovered through his insurance business that many of his clients were dying in their mid-forties, so he sold his property and his business and placed the money in investments. The first two years of retirement were wonderful, but as the next two years went by, the temptation to drink a little bit too much began to grow. With every day devoted solely to leisure, it started to become a little boring. Then one or two of the investments went wrong, inflation took hold, the cost of living rocketed and his income fell dramatically.

As he found it boring to party, go boating and swim each day, he decided to spend six months of the year in Andorra skiing. Well, after two years of being able to snow-ski every day in the winter, this also lost its glitter and it was easier not to bother to put the skis on. Then a few more investments did not work out as well as had been predicted.

To cut a long story short, he made the courageous decision to come back to the United Kingdom and recommence his career at the age of 50.

There is a valuable message here for us, and one for which I am personally grateful. First, too much of anything, even good things, destroys our happiness. Secondly, it is difficult to know how much money we truly need to fund our retirement lifestyle – we never know how long our lives will be. Also, one of the great troubles with retirement is that you can never take a day off! My friend CJ found that although he appeared to have amassed enough money, not only was it not enough, but just spending it on pleasure was not satisfying and did not bring happiness.

The balance of life is what is vital to success and happiness in amassing money. If you understand the dangers of chasing the goal of money for itself, then you can focus your efforts on the reasons why you desire to amass money.

SPENDING MONEY

It is what you spend your money on that is going to provide pleasure and happiness. You may spend the money on charities, helping others, you may spend the money on personal possessions and acquisitions, you may spend the money on travel and holidays, books or music, theatre, cinema, sports, motor cars or planes. You may just want to have the comfortable feeling of security that comes from having sufficient saved for the 'just in case' occasion. Whatever the reasons, there is enormous value in making money for the right principles.

Can just having money really give you pleasure? Of course not, but it can provide security. It may provide a better self-image, enhanced confidence. It can create so much good in the world when it is used wisely and, of course, it can contribute towards greater happiness, pleasure and enjoyment when the spending of money takes place in accordance with the three principles of happiness stressed throughout this book:

1. something to look forward to;
2. sharing;
3. making someone else happy.

MAKING YOUR FORTUNE

So let us now begin the process – first, developing a positive mindset, and secondly, finding the right technique.

Developing a positive mindset to make money

Once you have developed the right attitude for amassing money, it will be more valuable to you than any 'get-rich-quick' scheme or so-called gold-mine. Most mines run out at some stage and get-rich-quick schemes are often here today and gone tomorrow, while the right attitude is something that cannot be taken away, something that you can call on whenever you need it.

1. Don't chase money – chase success

Apply the law that says do not chase money, chase success. It is quite extraordinary how, when someone desperately needs money, and they wilfully and determinedly set out to get it by whatever means, money seems to run away, and vice versa.

This is also a characteristic of all the self-made millionaires and billionaires, who never set out to chase money – instead, their goal was success in many different forms. Some have been driven by the desire to create an empire; others by the wish to create a better life for their family or their children.

In the profession of selling, I have for years emphasized to those whose earnings are commission based the importance of never chasing the commission. Having pound signs in the eyes is readily spotted by a potential customer!

Commissioned salespeople always earn more when they set out to provide good service and products that the customers really want, rather than push on them items that pay the highest commission.

So, the message here is to have as your goal a vision of what the money is for, and how it will eventually be spent.

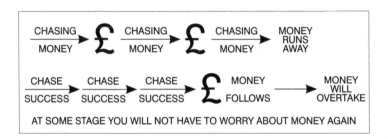

2. Build the right frame of mind

Build a secure frame of mind regarding money. What this really means is, be comfortable with money.

If you carry cash with you, be wary. Suppose you are going away on holiday and you have collected £1,000 from the bank – resist the temptation to show off your wads of currency as you pay for your taxi or tip the hotel porter. If you do, it will soon be stolen, or you will find that people will expect you to pay for all the drinks in the bar.

When, as is quite likely, you amass more money than your immediate friends or even your parents, do not feel uncomfortable or guilty. Obviously, though, you should avoid every temptation to brag and boast – this is vitally important as it can destroy relationships and, ultimately, destroy happiness.

One of my very good friends sold his business in his early forties, and received many millions of pounds. The first eight months after receiving this huge sum, he and his wife were really rather boring as it became their main topic of conversation. Every time we met, they would talk about what they could buy next or what they could spend their money on next, to such an extent that I started not to look forward to their company or their phone calls. Eventually, thank goodness, they realized that money is really quite a boring subject.

3. Conquer self-pity

Recognize that being without money or worrying about paying the bills, or even suffering some form of poverty, is a mindset, an attitude that allows one to be in that situation. It is totally curable. I am sure you know people who actually wallow in their own self-pity, who are almost frightened of money and of making money. They are most comfortable wanting to be dependent on others. Even if they were to have money they would not have the faintest idea of how to use it. To cure this condition, build up your desire to be self-sufficient and set goals that will lead you to that state.

4. Define what your money is for

Define in detail exactly what the money you are going to make is for. Your 'money goal' must be based on what the money is to achieve for you and for others, and not just an amount expressed in figures.

5. Visualize yourself with money

Visualize yourself with money. Build up a picture of yourself with money and see the lifestyle you will have and how you will feel, and develop your attitude to money so that it is positive.

6. Make the right affirmations

I am confident I have proved to you throughout this book that affirmations such as 'I am wealthy, I am financially secure' are a vital ingredient in achieving success.

Overcoming obstacles to making money

In order to amass money, you need first to make sure that you are not being held back, and secondly, to learn the basic techniques for making money.

1. Mix with the right people

Do not mix consistently with people who are unsuccessful as you will by now understand the consequences of environmental conditioning.

2. Don't use negative affirmations

Negative affirmations will guarantee negative results. Even if you are short of money, never say, 'I've never got any money, I'm always broke, I know I'll never have any.'

3. Don't make excuses

Do not make excuses: 'Well, it's impossible for me, I've got too many responsibilities, family, having to care for my partner', etc. Do not make excuses that you are in the wrong job, do not make excuses that there is just not enough time – the rich person has no more hours than the poor one.

4. Poverty is not a virtue

Do not kid yourself that there is any virtue is being poor. I find it so disagreeable that some sociologists or critical journalists try to persuade us of the virtue of poverty. The best possible future for those who are financially poor is that we do not all set out to join them. Those in the world who, for whatever reason, are hungry, destitute or needing help are surely dependent on those who generate success and wealth. Make no bones about it, there is no virtue in being penniless.

5. Be enthusiastic

Remove the mindset that has been implanted, no doubt through years of brainwashing, that in order to amass money one has to have a particular skill, education, qualification or intelligence. Understand that these are only 10 per cent of the qualifications needed – 90 per cent is down to attitude and self-management. There are so many people who have wonderful talents and gifts, but have no discipline. Just as important, remember that opportunities seem to avoid or miss people with a negative attitude. If you have a brilliant idea or an opportunity for making money, will you go and share it with somebody who will immediately set out to debunk or undermine it, or will you tell somebody who will be enthusiastic and as excited as you?

6. Control your expenses

As time goes by, do not let circumstances, position or ego keep you poor. It happens frequently that as people start to amass money, they spend too much too soon. As more money comes in, they cannot possibly wear the £25 shirt in the wardrobe; only a £125 shirt will do. The £200 suit definitely will not do; the suit now has to cost £1,200. It is quite extraordinary how people's expenses rise to meet their income, and many stay poor as a result.

7. Be careful how you lend money

Just one further word of caution. One of the surest ways of destroying your relationships is to lend money to a family connection, friend or acquaintance. This, in the vast majority of cases, ends in tears. Either the recipient does not regard paying back a relation or friend as important as repaying their bank or, because you are a friend, they even resent your request for the payback at the agreed time.

So, if tempted to lend, do not. Give if you wish to, but you will do no good to the other person or yourself by becoming a money-lender. Leave it to those who specialize in it.

The right techniques for making money

So, what we have done so far is to get the brain in gear and remove obstacles.

Now we come to the next stage: the specific application of the techniques and principles of amassing money.

1. Spend less than you earn

Why do so many people spend more than they earn? A typical example is the person who sets up his or her own business and does well straight away. In no time at all, that person has a new car, a new home, an expensive lifestyle and costly holidays – mostly funded on bank loans. To amass money you have to start out by spending less than you earn and keep doing so until you have amassed the amount you really need.

I have found that everyone who has amassed money practises this advice.

2. Save first, spend second

Save and put aside, say, 10 per cent of every pound that you earn. You can work the calculation out with compounded interest on the savings, but understand the basic principle of saving the 10 per cent first and spending the remainder afterwards. Most people do not do this. They pay the rent or mortgage, buy the food, spend money on whatever and then attempt to save what is left over. If you are truly determined to amass money, it is vital that saving is the first stage.

3. Make your money work for you

Money is a self-generator. It can be a multiplier, so spread your investments. Throughout history there have been stock market crashes every few years, from the current economic crisis to Black Monday in 1987 and back to the famous crashes of the 1930s. Those who survived those major depressions had their investments in a broad portfolio. In amassing money, you do not have to keep your savings in a monetary form. Investments can be in antiques, paintings, land, property, stamp collections, vintage motor cars and planes as well as in stocks and shares, gilts and equities, bonds and savings accounts.

4. Reinvest

If investments are properly placed and are working for you, they will provide an income. While you are in the process of amassing money, the income is, of course, not to be spent. That income should be reinvested, which will quite naturally speed up the process of making money.

5. Cut your losses

Cut your losses – FAST! I was very fortunate in learning a few brilliant tips from my stepfather, Victor Levy, who was a superb businessman and a great entrepreneur, as well as being a most charming person to be with. One of his favourite expressions was 'Cut your losses.' If a business deal went wrong or an investment was not doing well, he would go on with it only for so long before he would take action to sell, get out of or even give up on any venture that could be turning into a negative situation.

Many people waste time, energy and mental exertion trying to turn a loss into a profit.

A man bought a second-hand car for £4,300. He got it home and realized very quickly he did not like it, so immediately he tried to sell it. The best offer he received was £4,000. So, day after day he tried, through advertising, to get the price he wanted. He spent £210 on advertising and still had no buyer at £4,300. Some eight weeks later, now in total desperation, and having spent hours and hours on this fruitless exercise, he was finally forced to accept £3,900! What a waste of effort. If only he had cut his losses right at the very beginning, he would have had nearly all his money back and could have concentrated the creative part of his mind on how to make up the £300. Instead, he lost £400 between the selling price and buying price, £210 on advertising, and had weeks of frustration to boot.

Cut your losses and move on to the next challenge or opportunity.

6. Always buy quality

When you make purchases, always attempt to buy the very best quality you can afford. It seems really rather sad that people with very little money tend to buy cheap products. We all know the expression 'You get what you pay for', and in most cases we do. One of the characteristics, it seems, of those with old money is that they have cultivated this principle – the very best-quality cloth made into suits, or pairs of shoes that last for 30 to 40 years. You can apply this principle to most acquisitions, even though we are living in a very expendable society.

7. Mix with the successful

Mix, socialize and communicate with successful people. Their level of thinking and mindset is transferable and will rub off on you, and, just as importantly, opportunities to amass money will occur, because that is the world they are in. Their conversation cannot help but be partly concerned with money, and that is one reason why people who are already wealthy tend to become even wealthier.

8. Practice self-management

It seems that every wealthy person I have come across practises self-management, both consciously and subconsciously. Saving money requires self-control, so in order to accumulate great monetary wealth, you must manage your financial affairs carefully.

9. Spoil yourself occasionally

You need to have something to look forward to and you will accumulate more quickly with the occasional reward. So, by all means treat yourself to something worthwhile.

10. Look for opportunities

There are literally thousands of opportunities to make money facing you each day. Many people have amassed money by doing a weekend or evening job in addition to their regular one. You could even start your own business alongside your regular job or take the plunge and just run your own business full time. In my work, I meet huge numbers of people who, for a whole variety of reasons, have left 'big' business and have started their own companies. The opportunities to earn money for yourself are vast.

11. The more you give, the more you get

Finally, one further guaranteed technique of amassing money is the law of success: what you hand out in life, you get back with the chance of tenfold return. So, as you make money, give a proportion of it away, perhaps to good causes such as charities.

Pocket Reminders

Making money – developing the positive mindset:

1. Don't chase money – chase success
2. Build the right frame of mind
3. Conquer self-pity
4. Define what your money is for
5. Visualize yourself with money
6. Make the right affirmations.

Making money – overcoming obstacles:

1. Mix with the right people
2. Don't use negative affirmations
3. Don't make excuses
4. Poverty is not a virtue
5. Be enthusiastic
6. Control your expenses
7. Be careful how you lend money.

Making money – developing the right techniques:

1. Spend less than you earn

2. Save first, spend second

3. Make your money work for you

4. Reinvest

5. Cut your losses

6. Always buy quality

7. Mix with successful people

8. Practise self-management

9. Spoil yourself occasionally

10. Look for opportunities

11. The more you give, the more you get.

WISE WORDS

The be-all and end-all of life should not be to get rich but to enrich the world.

B C Forbes

MONEY-BACK GUARANTEE

I personally guarantee that if you apply the techniques from this book you will achieve greater wealth and happiness. In the extremely unlikely event that this should not happen, I will give you your money back.

Return this book, with your purchase receipt, within 30 days of purchase to the address below. You can also contact us for further information about books, audio cassettes, videos or live appearances:

The Richard Denny Group
1 Cotswold Link
Cotswold Business Village
Moreton-in-Marsh
Gloucestershire GL56 0JU

Tel: 01608 812424
Fax: 01608 651638
E-mail: success@denny.co.uk

Please visit our website at: www.denny.co.uk and get a FREE positive message every day on your computer to start the day with.

Richard Denny loves to hear from his readers, and particularly the successes they achieve having read his books and listened to his cassettes and CDs.